How to Care for Your Horse

Other Books by Jay Leech

Body in Elevator M
Cry of the Wolf
Bright Fawn and Me
Moon of the Big-Dog
Branded Runaway

How To Care For Your Horse

Jay Leech

PUBLICATIONS

MILLWOOD, NEW YORK 10546

Published 1983 by Breakthrough Publications Inc.,
Millwood, NY 10546

1st Printing 1979 by A.S. Barnes and Co., Inc.

Library of Congress Cataloging in Publication Data

Leech, Jay, 1931–
How to care for your horse.

Includes index.
1. Horses.　I.　Title.
SF285.3.L43　　　636.1'08　　　78-69635
ISBN 0-914327-02-X

Notice To Readers

The procedures and recommendations contained in this book should
be undertaken only with the proper professional supervision and
accordingly publisher takes no responsibility for the application of
the contents of this book including without limitation procedures,
theories, and product recommendations.

To all the beloved horses
who have endured many a human blunder
with nary the flick of an ear
in the process of transforming ordinary people into horsepeople.

Contents

Acknowledgments

I am grateful for the assistance and cooperation of the many people who so graciously assisted in making available the photographs and illustrations in this book.

My special appreciation goes to John Leech, an experienced horseman and agricultural extension agent of Michigan State University, who on many occasions went out of his way to be of assistance.

My thanks also go to Richard Rathke for his patience in drawing many of the technical illustrations.

I am indebted to Michigan State University's Large Animal Veterinary Clinic for making available the many photographs and illustrations of unsoundness and internal parasites and to the United States Department of Agriculture which furnished illustrations and technical information.

Last, but certainly not least, I express my loving appreciation to the other "bosses" on the farm, namely, Walt, Stef, and Lor, who so willingly throw their weight into the harness no matter what the load.

Jay Leech
Meadowcroft Farm
Durand, Michigan

Prayer of a Horse

To Thee, My Master, I Offer My Prayer:

Feed me, water and care for me, and when the day's work is done provide me with shelter, a clean dry bed and a stall wide enough for me to lie down in comfort. Talk to me. Your voice often means as much to me as the reins.

Pet me sometimes, that I may serve you the more gladly and learn to love you.

Do not jerk the reins, and do not whip me when going up hill.

Never strike, beat, or kick me when I do not understand what you want, but give me a chance to understand you. Watch me, and if I fail to do your bidding, see if something is not wrong with my harness or feet.

Examine my teeth when I do not eat. I may have an ulcerated tooth, and that, you know, is very painful.

Do not tie my head in an unnatural position, or take away my best defense against flies and mosquitoes by cutting off my tail, or limit my range of vision by blinders so that I am frightened by what I cannot see.

And finally, O my master, when my youthful strength is gone, do not turn me out to starve or freeze, or sell me to some cruel owner to be slowly tortured and starved to death; but do thou, my master, take my life in the kindest way, and your God will reward you here and hereafter.

You will not consider me irreverent if I ask this in the name of Him who was born in a stable. Amen.

Author Unknown
Sunday *Record-Herald*
Chicago, Illinois
March 3, 1912

How to Care for Your Horse

1
Do You Really Want a Horse?

Few horse lovers are fortunate enough to have been born and raised on a horse farm where they learned to ride and to care for a horse before they learned to walk. The vast majority of us had to yearn through those childhood years, content to watch the lucky girl down the road who had a pony to ride or to see Trigger alongside Roy Rogers in the movies or to go to the library and read every horse book we could get our hands on.

How we suffered with Black Beauty as the once elegant horse endured the degradations and cruelty of a pitiless master. How we agonized, wishing that somehow we could rescue the beautiful creature and take him home and love him.

However, if by some feat of magic one of us had managed to rescue Black Beauty and had taken him home, the results probably would have been disastrous. With as much factual knowledge as we had at the time relative to horse care, the elegant equine undoubtedly would have been in tragic circumstances. As much as we might have loved him, most of us would not have had the slightest idea of how to take care of him. Feeding him the other half of our peanut butter sandwich or tucking him away in a cardboard box in the corner simply would not have done the job.

Queen Anne's Lace. Pencil drawing by Gail Williams. Courtesy Walter L. Leech.

The purpose of this book is to help convert the mere horse lover into a knowledgeable horseperson. The real horseperson knows the needs of a horse and how to meet them. He or she knows how a horse thinks and will react, how to communicate with a horse and how to make the commands known so that the horse can obey. Simply being the owner of a horse does not automatically make a horseperson. Nor does simply reading a book make the reader knowledgeable. But this book can help by making you aware of the horse's needs, and aware of his actions and reactions. Once you know your horse, you will know what he is going to think before he thinks it. By the same reasoning, your horse will know you.

It is interesting to note that most horse people are also dog people and cat people—or any-animal people for that matter—so they usually have a built-in feel for animals. To verify this, all you have to do is walk through the stabling area of any horse show and see pets of every description. You will likely see a pet goat that simply could not be left at home by himself, or a starving stray puppy that another horseperson rescued in the parking lot, or an exhibitor with a basketful of two-day-old motherless kittens that require bottle feeding between classes.

Not all people who own horses are good horsepersons. Fortunately, it is relatively easy to spot bad ones. If the general condition of the horse is poor, if the owner jerks and slaps the horse around or uses loud abusive language, this is almost a sure indicator that you are witnessing a poor horseperson in action. Good horsepersons shy away from such people. They want nothing to do with him or his kind. Certainly, no one seeking advice or information on horses should seek it from this sort of person. Advice from a poor horseperson is infinitely worse than no advice at all.

If only one word could be used to describe a good horseperson, that word would not be love or compassion or experience. All of these qualities are excellent, but they are not enough. The single word would be *responsible*, and it covers a multitude of things. A horse is a live, feeling animal. He bleeds when he is cut. He shivers when he is cold. His stomach hurts when he is hungry. He requires and deserves a responsible owner to care for him.

Time and time again the unfortunate results are evident when an irresponsible person decided that he simply must have a horse. How tragic for the animal when that person also decides that a horse really is not what he wants at all. A horse requires too much time and too much care, and the ego-trip he thought he would get from the horse just is not worth the effort.

Anyone who has witnessed the heartbreaking rescue of animals suffering the dire consequences of inhumane and irresponsible owners will never be able to forget the experience. Some of these pathetic victims are afflicted with the results of neglect and malnutrition to the extent that they are not capable of walking or even taking nourishment. Others are fur-covered skeletons riddled with disease. With painstaking care some of these animals eventually recover to the point of being serviceable. Unfortunately, many are beyond help and have to be humanely destroyed.

17

The honest fact of the matter is, horses do require care, and care necessarily involves time and work. No horseman worthy of that name would consider sitting down at his own dinner table before his horse has been tended and fed.

As long as we are talking very frankly about responsibility, let us also talk about cost, because it would be ridiculous to think that the care of a horse does not also involve money. Just how much money is needed depends on the area in which you live and where and how you intend to keep your horse. If you are fortunate enough to live on adequate acreage and have the facilities to keep the horse at home, the cost of course, will be less than if you must pay board to a professional stable.

Attempting to state actual sums is next to impossible in this day of rapidly escalating prices, but let's try it anyway. At least you will have some idea of what the cost might be.

A boarding stable can run anywhere from $60 to $200 per month and even more if you live in a highly urbanized area. In addition to board you must figure on an occasional veterinarian's bill. Many veterinarians charge a fee for a stable call (this may run $10 to $30 and then charge an additional fee for the service that is rendered. This cost is highly variable from area to area and from veterinarian to veterinarian.

Another cost which must be figured is the regular visit from the farrier, roughly once every six weeks to two months. Trimming the horse's hooves will probably cost somewhere from $8 to $14; resetting shoes (this includes trimming), $20 to $30; and plain shoeing (this also includes trimming), $25 to $35.

Keeping the abovementioned facts and figures in mind, if you are considering the purchase of a horse, also consider the following as a horse owner:

1. Are you prepared to provide a proper diet for your horse?
2. Are you willing to provide proper hoof care for your horse?
3. Are you willing to see to it that your horse is fed and has fresh water at least twice a day, seven days a week, 365 days a year?
4. Are you willing to see to it that your horse gets veterinarian care if and when he may need it?
5. Are you willing to see that your horse is properly and safely stabled?
6. Are you willing to exercise your horse or see to it that he has a pasture or paddock where he can exercise himself?

If your honest answer to any one of the above questions is no, *Then Don't Get A Horse.* Get a motorcycle or a pair of roller skates. Get anything, but don't get a horse.

On the other hand, if your answers are all a solid yes, then welcome to the world of horses and horse people.

We have a saying, "The outside of a horse is good for the inside of a man." An old horseman friend put the identical meaning in his own words: "There ain't nothin' about a horse that ain't good for a body."

To the horseperson who has real affection for his horse, the work of caring for him is gladly, even eagerly, given. The mundane chores of keeping fresh water in the horse's bucket, feeding him, or cleaning his stall are just excuses to be out at the barn. The barn is a peaceful place, removed from the pressure world in which most of us live. For the time that you are totally involved with your horse there is, almost miraculously, no room for the worries and problems that might be nagging at you. There is only room for you and your beautiful animal. You smell the sweet, rich odor of him, touch the satin sleekness of his summer coat, feel the velvet soft muzzle as it nudges you affectionately.

When you ride, his strong muscles move with power beneath you, and you are swept along above the ground in exhilarating motion. You are outdoors breathing fresh air, enjoying the grandeur of nature that is all around you. When you are riding or working with your horse, seldom-used muscles are put into play and you derive the benefit of healthful exercise.

Once you have owned a great horse, be it a pleasure hack, a working stock horse, or a show horse, you will receive the joy-giving experience that will be hard to surpass anywhere. And in no way can it be measured in dollars and cents.

2
Purchasing the First Horse

When purchasing his or her first horse, the inexperienced horse person should not be hasty. It is very easy to fall in love with a weanling filly or a blossoming two-year old colt, and too frequently the inclination to "bundle them up and take them home" has been acted upon.

By way of explanation, there is absolutely nothing wrong with a sweet weanling filly or a blossoming two-year old colt—quite the contrary. Each in his own way is very rewarding and challenging to the experienced horseperson. To the novice who needs the benefit of learning from the horse, the best advice is "stay away from the youngsters," charming as they may be. The young horse needs an experienced handler every bit as much as the novice owner needs an experienced horse. It is easy to ruin a young horse by making mistakes and to frighten a good prospective horseperson by mounting him on an untrained animal.

Therefore, here is some general advice that may be of benefit to beginners: your first horse should be from six to ten years old (even older if he is in good physical condition), sound, of a quiet nature, and well settled in his training. The fact that a horse is smooth-mouthed (a horse nine years old or older) is not a detriment when purchasing an animal. In fact, many a champion horse has some age on him. If an aged horse has good sound feet, legs, and teeth, he more than likely has many years of good service to offer; as a pleasure mount he will be hard

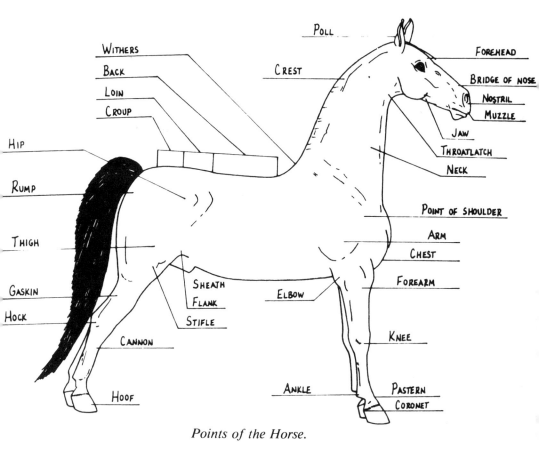

POLL

WITHERS

FOREHEAD

BACK

CREST

BRIDGE OF NOSE

LOIN

NOSTRIL

CROUP

MUZZLE

HIP

JAW

THROATLATCH

NECK

RUMP

POINT OF SHOULDER

ARM

THIGH

CHEST

FOREARM

GASKIN

SHEATH

ELBOW

FLANK

HOCK

STIFLE

KNEE

CANNON

ANKLE

PASTERN

HOOF

CORONET

Points of the Horse.

to beat. The aged horse that has been carefully and well used is not easily spoiled by a beginner. He will respond consistently, and if the rider will watch carefully how his horse responds when he does certain things, he can quickly learn much about riding. Keep in mind that the horse is much wiser about many matters than is the neophyte rider.

This in no way implies that there have not been young horses that have taught amateurs to ride and given them years of good service. But the odds favor the side of the aged horse as the superior mount.

To find the kind of horse most suitable for the beginner is not an easy task. Answering ads in the newspapers can be a gamble unless you have an experienced horseperson inspect the animal before making a purchase.

The most likely place to find a good first horse is in a club or commercial stable of the right type. A stable that takes on all comers and turns them loose to ride or fall off is not likely to have a horse suitable for a personal mount. Look for a stable of good reputation that lets horses out only under close supervision.

There are horse auctions all over the country for both grade and pure bred animals offering good using horses. But the amateur should always have a competent horseperson with him to check the animal thoroughly before sale time.

The prospective buyer also may study the better horse magazines. There you can acquaint yourself with the names of reliable breeders and trainers. A letter stating your price range and giving a general description of the sort of animal you are looking for may bring a useful answer, or at least a suggestion.

An inquiry placed with various breed associations also could be of help. All breeds of horses have a national registry for their pure bred stock. And since horses are their business, they will be willing to offer help to a prospective buyer. (The addresses of these registry associations are listed at the back of this book.)

In selecting a horse, the first consideration should be given to whether or not the prospective horse is suitable for the purpose for which it will be used.

Assuming that the horse has been found that appeals to the eye, the animal should be observed in his stall as he stands relaxed. The sound horse should stand with all four feet under and in equal support of the body. If he frequently shifts the position of the feet, cocks a hind leg, stands with one forefoot pointed, or if either or both knees tremble or seem loose, this might indicate some soreness, unsoundness, or other disabling condition. Regardless of any other attributes a horse may have, a horse is no better than his feet and legs.

A horse with a cough might indicate only a simple sore throat. However, it might indicate heaves, asthma, or a predisposition to heaves or other throat or lung ailments.

If a horse wears a collar around his throat, this might be simply a jowl sweat strap, an item commonly worn by show horses to keep the throat and jowl trim. On the other hand, the horse might be a cribber, and the collar might be a cribbing strap. Observe the stall closely in the areas around the grainbox or other ledges for evidence of much wood biting. Cribbing can be a habit that is merely annoying to the listener, but it also can lead to wind sucking and attacks of colic.

A horse that paces laterally in his stall or stands and shifts his weight in a swinging motion from side to side is a weaver. A weaver's stall usually can be identified by a wide path worn down in the area where he weaves.

If the prospect is wearing a stable sheet or blanket and also is wearing a leather bib or muzzle attached to the halter, this possibly indicates that he tears and pulls at his blanket.

If the horse is wearing a length of chain attached to his hind ankles, this probably indicates that he kicks in the stall. If many stall boards are broken or splintered, this also could indicate a kicker.

A horse may give evidence of abuse by swinging away or being apprehensive when his head is approachd or his feet are picked up.

After you have observed the animal in the stall, have him brought outside. Take plenty of time to look him over well. The horse should be in good flesh and general good physical condition, his coat smooth with a sheen of health to it. Leave the business of buying an out-of-condition horse that may turn a profit when in good flesh to the professional. If the horse is thin and poor, he may be a hard keeper, or there may be even more serious problems.

The nostrils should be clean, free of any mucous discharge. A runny nose could be the result of a simple cold, but it also could indicate a more serious or chronic problem.

The eyes should come under close scrutiny. They should be large and prominent. A small pig-eye sometimes is an indication of poor temperament. The eyes should present a clear, bright, intelligent appearance, free from any cloudiness. A watering eye should cause suspicion.

The owner of an Arabian horse highly prizes the "dish" in his animal's face. This refined concave bone structure is characteristic of the Arabian breed. However, with this exception the face should be

Ideal Face.

Bulging Face.   *Dish Face.*

straight with cleanly chizzled lines, free of a "dish" or bulge. The horse should be broad between the eyes, long from the line of the eye to the top of the head, with plenty of room between the base of the ears. The jowl should not be heavy nor the throatlatch thick.

Is there good distance between the front legs where they come out of the breast? Your flattened hand should fit in this area easily. There is serious objection to horses that are too narrow in the front. It indicates weakness, and probably he will be subject to interference when he moves. Still giving attention to the front legs, does he toe in or toe out? Is he bowlegged, pigeon-toed, knock-kneed? All of these faults are objectionable because they can interfere with a clean way of going.

Move around to the rear and study his hind legs. Is he bowlegged or cow-hocked? Does he stand too close or too wide? Is the hind leg too straight? Does he stand under? Is he camped out?

The horse should stand on good clean legs free of puffs or swellings. Run a hand down each front leg, feeling for splints or other enlargements. Feel around the coronet area for ring bone or side bone. Make the same examination of the hind legs, giving special attention to the area around the hocks for spavin. Are the hocks clean and well defined, or are they rounded, indicating curb or caps?

The hoof should appear round at the ground. The walls of the feet should be smooth and free of cracks. The hoof, as it is attached to the pastern, should form a continuous line to the ground. Pick up the foot.

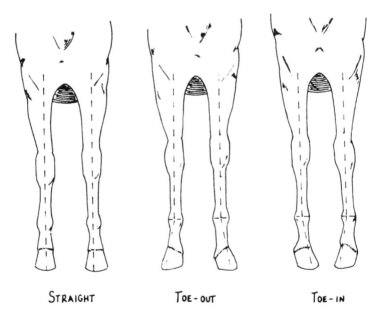

STRAIGHT   TOE-OUT   TOE-IN

Ideal and Faulty Conformation of the Front Legs.

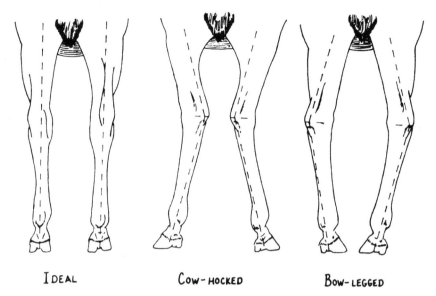

I DEAL   COW-HOCKED   BOW-LEGGED

Ideal and Faulty Conformation of the Hind Legs.

If it feels hot to the touch, this could indicate thrush or other inflamation.

If the horse appeals to you after observing him in his stall and giving closer examination, have the horse ridden. From all angles observe how the horse moves at the various gaits. Have a clear mental picture of the ideal movement in each gait, and observe how closely the horse comes to that idea of perfection.

After observing the horse being ridden (or driven), ride the horse yourself. Take particular note of how the horse feels as he executes the gaits. Are the gaits smooth? Does the horse seem to enjoy his work? Are his ears up and alert? Does he move freely? Does he seem fractious or balky? Does he take his gaits readily? Is he difficult to keep in any gait? Does his mouth respond to a light touch, or does he lug or pull?

Will the horse load in a trailer? Even if at the present time you do not expect to haul him, you may at some future date want to take him to a horse show or join a trail riders clubs. It may be necessary to haul him to a farrier to be shod or to a large animal clinic for medical attention. Every modern horse must be willing to go into a trailer or horse van and ride quietly. Once a horse is spoiled in this regard, he is hard to correct.

Do not feel shy or self-conscious about asking any pertinent questions that come to mind relative to the horse or his habits. Your questions do not indicate ignorance, as some novice horsepeople fear. Quite the contrary, they indicate your interest in the animal, and a reliable seller will answer them gladly and honestly.

If the prospect has met your requirements, it is important to take note of the way the horse is bitted. Note not only the type of bits, but how they are positioned in the horse's mouth. Is the curb chain or strap loose or fairly snug? If possible, purchase the bridle and bits that the horse has been wearing. If not, obtain equipment identical to those to which the horse is accustomed.

Of necessity, the foregoing comments are limited in scope and touch upon only some things to be considered when you are purchasing a horse. To be on the safe side, a thorough examination for soundness and health should be made by a competent horse veterinarian. The charge for this service will represent money well spent and can prevent a great deal of future grief and disappointment. Generally, any reputable seller interested in disposing of a good horse that is sound will have no objection to allowing a reasonable trial period to a responsible buyer.

The wise buyer will go to a reputable breeder or dealer who will guarantee the horse to be as represented at the time of the sale. The wise buyer also will expect to pay a fair price for a good horse.

There's a saying heard frequently around horsepeople: it doesn't cost any more to keep a good horse than it does to keep a poor horse. And that's a fact. So take the time required to buy that "good" horse.

3
Your Relationship with Your Horse

Discussions about horses frequently include references to their limited intelligence. On the intelligence scale, as computed by scientists, the horse ranks somewhere between fourth and tenth, behind the ape, the elephant, and the dog. In human terms this is probably so, insofar as there have been no reports of horses reputed to be successful in mastering the intricacies of calculus and the Nobel prize for literature has yet to be awarded to an equine.

However, many knowledgeable horsepeople oppose the idea that simply because the horse cannot read, write, or do arithmetic, he is limited in intelligence. They are convinced that he has facilities of perception and emotional subtleties as far beyond the human understanding as calculus is beyond the horse's comprehension.

To the professional handler or trainer whose attitude toward the horse is usually strictly business, the matter of intelligence is of little importance. His relationship is on a nonpersonal, work-profit basis. The horse is treated as a valuable piece of property, no more, no less. When the horse is tacked up, out on the track, or in the ring for his daily workout, the horse knows that work is the order of the day. However, both professional and amateur trainers could profit by occasionally taking stock of the nature of the horse's intelligence as well as his emotional needs.

Most horsepeople agree that the horse understands only a few spoken words. However, this most certainly is not the limit of his comprehension. The number of words that he actually understands may be few, but he understands well the tone of voice. What he seems to comprehend best is the total demeanor of the people around him. In other words, he seems able to "read" the total person rather than only part of him.

The horse knows instantly if his handler is confident or unsure, and more often than not he will react accordingly. If the handler is fearful, the horse will "pick this up" and in turn be fearful. Frequently the novice handler misinterprets this reaction as aggression. If the rider tightens his muscles in anticipation of trouble, the horse responds to this impulse and at once looks around, searching for the source of the fear that is being transmitted to him. At this point he will accept almost anything as the source of the fear: a bird fluttering in the bushes or a gust of wind rustling in the trees—and he is ready to bolt.

In understanding the horse, you must also understand his nature and instincts. In the wild the horse's most effective defense against predators is his speed. Therefore, when he detects danger of any sort, his first instinct is to run. If all avenues of escape are cut off, the horse will stand and fight and do a good job of it. But with the horse fighting is secondary; his first line of defense is his swiftness of foot.

The horse, as in his human counterpart, has two brain lobes. However, unlike humans, there apparently is little connection between the lobes of the horse's brain. Therefore, he is referred to as having "two-sides." For this reason it is necessary to educate both sides of the horse for the same thing. For instance, a horse that is used to being saddled only from the left side may be startled if suddenly a saddle is slapped on him from the right. It is necessary to train both the right side and the left side, almost independently of each other.

The horse has an uncanny memory. It can be likened to the proverbial memory of the elephant. That's one reason it is so important to use extreme care in the training of the horse. Once he has established a "good" memory imprint, it is more than likely going to stick. The same is true of a "bad" memory imprint. Once a horse has been spoiled by poor handling or training, or a bad experience of whatever nature, it is very difficult (sometimes impossible) to train it out of him.

Very rarely is a horse born malicious. As a youngster he is charming, curious, and timid. If he turns out to be a bad actor, you can almost be assured that he has been made that way by poor handling.

In the earliest stages of training it is only natural that the horse resent restrictions on his personal liberty. Understanding the horse's basic reaction to a totally new and possibly frightening situation is a must. When a horse is first handled, he very likely may resist. This resistance is caused partly through anger at being restricted and partly through fear of something he cannot understand. It is at this point that extreme care and patience are required of the trainer. However, once the horse understands what is required of him, in most cases he is quite philosophical and willing to accept the inevitable demands made upon him by man.

The wise and prudent horseperson will give sufficient thought to introducing a horse to a new experience before he attempts it. If a colt is ideally trained, he need never know fear of people. The perfect mount is not a fearful horse. He is a responsive horse.

The horse evolved as a herd animal. Therefore, he is instinctively familiar with a structured social order. Each herd has its leader, the herd stallion. Second to him is the herd mare. She is usually an older mare, strong, tough, and wise in the ways of survival. Beneath that top level of leadership comes the rest of the herd, which is not simply a "lump" of horses. Within the herd itself, there is a pecking order in which decisions are made such as who is permitted to drink first at the watering hole or who gets the choicest patch of grass. This order is determined by the strength and aggressiveness of the individual horse. The timid, weaker horse (or inexperienced youngsters) will be at the bottom of this order. The stronger, bolder horse will be high in this order.

Each horse knows his established position in the herd. He will stay in that position only as long as he can successfully defend it from the challenges of the horses beneath him. He can move up the ladder by successfully challenging the horse above him.

The equine social order is discussed here for the purpose of better understanding the horse's basic nature and his relationship with you as his owner-trainer-handler. It is important that you establish yourself in the horse's mind as being above him in the social order. If he lays his ears back at you or stomps his foot and you back off, in his mind you have become his inferior and are subject to do as he wishes. In horse terms *you* stand back at the watering hole and wait while he gets his drink first.

It is the rare horse that will not test his owner-handler-trainer. His way may be so subtle that you hardly notice, but have no doubt, the horse is taking careful note of your response. For this reason the handler's reaction must always be positive.

If you are a novice horseperson, do not construe a positive action to be a foolish one. If you encounter an incorrigible horse that threatens to be a physical danger to you, don't be dumb. Get out of the way! Leave a bad actor to someone who is more experienced and capable of handling the situation.

What we're talking about here are the small, harmless tests that almost any horse will try, just to see where he stands.

For instance, let's assume that you are leading your horse on the driveway back to the barn. The horse sees an inviting patch of green grass and decides he would like to eat some. So he pulls you off the driveway, contrary to your wishes, and proceeds to eat. You then have to physically drag the horse away.

The time for you to have been aware of the horse's intent was back when the thought first crossed his mind. The indicators might have been only a slight glance at the grass, a turn of his head, or a wavering of his step. That was the time for you to reaffirm your wish to go directly to the barn. This might have required only a spoken word, a slight touch on the lead line, or perhaps a sharper snap of the lead line (this will depend on the basic nature of the individual horse). Once he has already made his move and dragged you over to the grass, you have been tested and had and the horse has come out the winner.

Using the same situation, let's assume that your reaction was the opposite: you were in no hurry and the day was lovely and warm and, if you had thought of it first, more than likely you would have offered to stop and let the horse graze for a while. Your proper reaction would have been to halt, or half-halt, and then affirmatively lead the horse to the grass, giving him the impression that it was your idea all along.

In the first instance the horse is in command of the situation. In the second instance, you are in command. The incident may seem trivial, and the line is a fine one. But it is an important one if you wish to maintain your position above the horse on his "social ladder."

In dealing with and educating the horse, you are encountering an animal of unbounded strength. Certainly, you are no physical match for him. However, you have the better of it, because the horse has been taken out of his natural environment and placed into yours. You have the advantage of being on your own ground, and you can think and reason. Your job as owner-trainer-handler is to substitute your will for the horse's will and to keep him under sufficient submission for control.

In equine vernacular you often hear the term "breaking the horse." The term is offensive to many horsepeople because it carries with it the wrong connotation. A "broken" horse or a horse with a crushed spirit is useless. You want a horse that works with you and for you, just as you work with and for the horse. You want all his brilliance and nerve and spirit intact, and you want it to be yours for the asking. You want him to nicker to you when he hears you coming to the stable, not to sulk in the corner of his stall or to turn from you in fear. When you call him in the pasture, you want him to gallop to you eagerly, not to run to the farthest corner in an attempt to hide or get away. You want him sensitive to your needs and desires, just as you are sensitive to his. Neither of you run roughshod over the other. You respect each other as individual creatures, with you doing your part and the horse doing his.

Your horse cannot comply with your wishes or demands until he understands them. With you as the so-called "superior" being, it is your job to see to it that he does understand. After all, why should you expect the horse to understand you if you do not understand him? The better you understand your horse and what makes him tick, the more you will be able to get a full measure of joy from him and with him.

The ideal relationship between a horse and "his person" is one of mutual trust and affection. This relationship is not one that is developed only when the saddle is placed on his back and the rider is mounted. Quite the contrary, it is developed day by day, in a slow and steady process. Each time you approach and have contact with your horse you leave an imprint on his memory, and that imprint is reinforced. The routine tasks of taking care of the personal mount can, and should, accomplish more than simply providing for the horse's physical needs. It is the most basic and effective way of truly getting to know your horse.

An impersonal, machine-like relationship can be achieved by a person who takes a horse in hand with the feeling that man is the superior creature who must dominate and control by whatever means necessary, including force. However, there has been many an occasion when a rider has been thankful that there was more than a "machine-like relationship" involved between him and his mount. The following story will serve to make the point.

A young woman purchased her first horse, a weanling American Saddlebred filly. Other than riding livery stable horses a few times, she knew nothing about horses except that she loved them and had to have one of her own. With what knowledge she could get from a book, the young woman undertook the step-by-step training of her filly. Admittedly, she made more than her fair share of mistakes, but nonetheless she established a sensitive two-way relationship with her little mare.

When the filly was a three-year-old and hardly more than green-trained, the owner foolishly decided that a ride across the countryside was in order. The ride started quietly enough, but as the little filly got the feel of the "fun of it" and viewed the new sights and open space in front of her, her pace steadily quickened. The relaxed amble moved to a trot, the trot to a canter, and the canter into a full gallop. The filly was having the time of her life, but the rider was in no way in control of the situation. She was only valiantly hanging on and attempting to stay in the saddle.

As they bounded full tilt between the rows of a cornfield, the filly obviously decided that a bite of the long green leaves would make a tasty mouthful. In order to grab that bite on the run she was forced to break stride. That momentary break was all it took to finish unseating the rider. It sent her catapulting over the filly's shoulder to the ground, directly in the path of the horse's hooves.

In the split second that it took to happen, the young horse, who had never had an experience such as this before, pulled herself from a full gallop to a dead stop. There she stood motionless. For several moments the owner lay stunned. When her senses returned and she opened her eyes, she was greeted with a worm's eye view of the underside of her horse. She was flat on her back between her filly's legs. If the horse had taken one more step, she could not have avoided crushing her mistress.

Just luck? Some people might say so, but this young owner definitely is not one of those people. She will insist to her dying breath that her filly "knew" and cared enough to stop.

The conscientious owner might well bear in mind that since the horse is by nature a herd animal, he thrives best in the company of other horses. He will frequently become dull and listless in forced isolation. However, in some cases his reaction may be quite the opposite. Such as was the case of a five-year-old pleasure gelding.

This horse had a good disposition, had been carefully handled, and had been ideally trained as a pleasure mount. His new owner had done all the right things. He had purchased the bridle along with the horse and spent thirty days handling and riding his new horse under the supervision of the horse's trainer. He had carefully remodeled a small shed and fenced a large grassy area for a paddock. Everything was right until the horse got to his new home.

Suddenly, this "perfect" mount was frantically pawing gaping holes in the floor of his stall, throwing his grain to the ground, and stomping it in the dirt. He paced his stall constantly, rarely sleeping, whinnying and screaming long into the night. When his new owner went into the stall to reassure the horse, he was met with a fretful bundle of nerve and muscle that no amount of reassurance could calm. This novice horseman was frightened, and rightly so because in the horse's present state, he was in no condition to be reasonable.

To a knowledgeable horseperson, the problem would have been obvious. From the time he was born, the gelding had been with a herd. Suddenly he was alone, and he could not adjust to the loneliness.

The new owner was genuinely fond of his horse and wanted to keep him if the problem could be solved. It was, and very easily. With the addition of a pony, the gelding was content. He had his "herd" again.

No two horses are like, just as no two people are alike. Whether the horse-owner relationship is tender and sentimental or all business, there is a strong common factor that is essential to the favorable horse response. A professional horseman renowned in the horse industry for many years put it this way: "Never lie to a horse. He won't never forget it."

In other words, let the horse know what to expect. For him there is a reason for everything that happens. Do not establish one sort of relationship, leading him to believe you are one kind of person, and then suddenly trick him by doing and being something totally different.

This does not mean that the owner should not expect his or her horse to enter into whims and moods occasionally. All creatures do, including people. What it means is that you should know your horse and let him know you. Then you can respond to his moods, and he can respond to yours.

4
Stabling the Horse

Whether your stable is new and built-to-order or is a converted shed or garage, its purpose is the same: to modify winter and summer temperatures, maintain acceptable humidity and ventilation, and protect horses from the ravages of excessive rain, snow, sun, and wind. Your horse should have comfortable quarters, but they need not be expensive or elaborate. However, an attractive well-kept barn certainly adds to the beauty of the landscape, and a clean stable indicates pride in ownership, to say nothing of increasing the value of your property.

Whether elaborate or simple, there are some requisites all horse barns should meet:

1. Barns should be on high ground so water will drain away from them.
2. Barns should be well ventilated.
3. Feeding and watering equipment should be arranged so that attendants need not walk behind the horses.
4. Feed storage areas should be free of rodents, birds, and *horses*.
5. Any projections that might injure horses should be removed.
6. Barns should be easy to keep clean so that they will provide healthful living conditions. A healthy horse is a better performer and an easier "keeper."
7. Any small swinging door through which the horse is to pass must be provided with a catch to hold it open. Many a hip has been broken by a door swinging shut when a horse is entering.
8. There must be no exposed electrical wiring in the stall. Horses are

playful, and they are curious. They also are highly susceptible to electricity. The charge from a light socket or 110-volt wire can kill a horse.

9. Use secure latches on stall doors, paddock and pasture gates.

10. Keep stable and fencing in good repair to lessen the hazard of injury.

The type of stabling your horse requires will depend a large part on the following:

1. The climactic conditions in the region of the country in which you live.
2. The kind of use required of your horse.
3. The amount of money you wish to spend.

A farm shed or garage can readily be converted into a very adequate stable facility by any reasonably handy amateur carpenter. However, if grain cannot be kept behind a closed door in a service or tack room, make a strong box with a lid that the horse cannot open.

Some owners use a double precaution. The grain is kept in a grain room behind a door that opens out so that the horse cannot push it open with his nose. Inside the grain room the grain is stored in a large bin with a hinged lid equipped with a latch and bolt.

The ways by which a horse can manage to get into the grain are many and varied, and most of them result in a seriously ill horse.

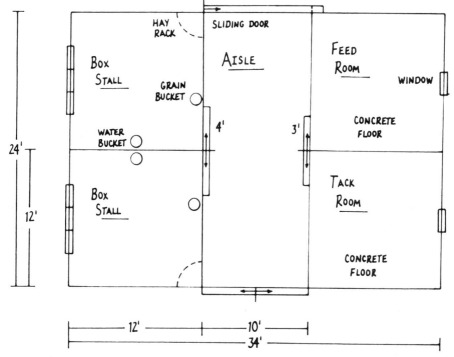

Floor plan of a small, but comfortable and efficient horse barn.

THE STALL

The stall should be airy and light. If space permits, a box stall of 16 x 16 feet is ideal, although 12 x 12 is adequate. Rough-cut hardwood 2 inches thick makes excellent stall partitions and lining. Avoid soft wood for this purpose because most horses have a tendency to chew and eat soft wood like stick candy. The partition should be solid to the height of at least 5 feet. Above that level you may wish to have it slotted for better ventilation. Chain link fencing or other heavy gauge fencing can be satisfactorily used for upper level partitions. Care should be taken to place the partitions all the way to the floor, leaving no crack beneath them. There have been many instances where a foot or leg has become wedged in such an opening with serious consequences.

BEDDING

A soft, comfortable bed will help ensure proper rest for your horse, as he will be more inclined to lie down and rest. He also will be much easier to groom if his bedding is kept clean. What you use for bedding will be dictated by availability and price. Basically, bedding should have good absorptive capacity and not be dusty. Cereal grain straw (oat and wheat) or wood shavings generally make the best material for bedding. Oat straw tends to be more absorbent. However, wheat straw is often preferred as the horse is less inclined to eat it.

THE FLOOR

A good floor can be made by using an 8 inch coarse gravel or cinder base topped with an 8-to-10-inch layer of tamped clay. The clay will pack, giving a firm floor, while the cinder or gravel beneath will hasten absorption of dampness. Your local supply will dictate what kind of material is available.

Whatever the material, the floor should be level. The nearer the floor comes to duplicating the natural conditions of sod, the better for the horse's legs and feet. The top layer of dirt or clay should be removed yearly and replaced with fresh dirt or clay, leveled, and then tamped.

MANGERS, FEED, AND WATER EQUIPMENT

The purpose of feed and water equipment is obvious. However, there are as many ideas about proper mangers and feed boxes as there are notions about horses. But when it's all said and done, the purpose remains the same. The feed box and manger are simply containers from which to feed the horse, and they should be constructed so that they do not provide a hazard to the animal.

The most popular type of manger is made of wood. Where rough-cut hard wood is available it is the best, because it is the most durable. The manger should be large enough for the horse to get his head into easily when he is feeding, and the part nearest the horse should be a few inches higher than the point of his shoulder. The bottom of the hay manger should be flat and smooth so it can be cleaned readily from time to time. Some horsepeople prefer to have the bottom slatted so that dust and chaff will sift out.

The grain box may be built in the upper part of the hay manger. It should be sufficiently deep to prevent the horse from throwing his grain out. For loose salt and minerals or a salt-mineral block, provide a little box narrower and shallower than the feed box. In lieu of a grain box, a pail or tub can be used.

A water bucket—made of metal, plastic, or rubber—with a capacity of 16 to 20 quarts also should be located at the front of the stall at a height of 38 to 42 inches.

VENTILATION

In hot climates, shelter from the sun is about all that is required. However, in climates where the winters are extremely cold, a more substantial shelter will be required. In cold areas there is a temptation to make the stable airtight. This will cause no harm if you are conscientious about airing the stable out daily and giving the horse an opportunity to be outside some time every day that the weather permits. A stable should have as little moisture and odor as possible. A 1,000-pound animal breathes approximately 2.1 gallons of moisture into the air per day. Without adequate ventilation, this much moisture can cause bronchial and lung ailments.

If your stable does not have a roof ventilating system, satisfactory summer ventilation can be achieved by opening barn doors and installing hinged walls or panels that swing open near the ceiling.

If the horse is kept in the stall most of the time, it is not unusual to get an odor buildup of ammonia from the horse's urine. Of course, regular cleaning will help minimize this, but occasionally you may wish to remove all the bedding, clean and rake the stall well, and then sprinkle the stall floor with agricultural lime. It should go without saying that when you have done this you must use care in rebedding the stall so that the horse does not come in contact with the lime.

PADDOCKS

A horse barn should have a well-drained, safe, fenced paddock (corral) adjacent to it. If this is not possible, the paddock should be nearby. A paddock can eliminate much of the work of grooming and stall cleaning as well as provide a place for your horse to get fresh air, sunshine, and exercise. There is no specified size or shape for a paddock. However, it should be of sufficient proportion to allow a horse to exercise himself freely. If given the choice of having a small square paddock or a long narrow one, the longer one is the definite preference. If space is a problem, a paddock of even 1,500 square feet will help a great deal.

Do Not Use Woven Wire Or Barbed Wire As Fencing Material For the Paddock. Use board fence, steel or aluminum rails or poles, or chain link.

FENCING

Woven wire: Large pastures may be fenced with woven wire if the concentration of horses is not too great. The mesh of the wire should be small so the horses cannot get their feet through it.

Barbed wire: Horsepeople usually avoid the use of barbed wire as a suitable fencing material, and the reason should be obvious.

Board fences: There's hardly a prettier sight in the world than a herd of horses on lush green pasture enclosed by white board fences. However, those beautiful board fences do have their drawbacks. Horses like to chew them, they splinter and break when they are kicked, and they have to be painted regularly.

Electrified wire: Homemade electric fence units should be avoided. A horse can stand very little current. Horses are so susceptible to electricity that many have been electrocuted by the current from a 110-volt socket. The best use of electric wire is in conjunction with other fencing material such as woven wire or board. In such cases the electric wire should be located *inside* the board or wire fence, installed on insulators according to the directions that come with the unit.

Electric fence chargers can be purchased at farm and feed stores or large hardware stores. Check the unit's specifications and be sure it is properly underwritten and safe for use with horses. Also available is a 6-volt battery-operated charger. These are excellent and perfectly safe for any equine.

The only disadvantage or danger from properly used and underwritten electrified wire comes if the current is off. Should the unit be accidentally unplugged or the wire broken or "shorted" for whatever

Post and fencing material	Post length and diameter	Size of rails, boards, or poles and gage of wire	Fence height	Number of rails, boards, or poles and mesh of wire	Distance between posts on centers
			Inches		*Feet*
Steel or aluminum posts and rails.[1]	7½ ft	10 or 20 ft. long	60	3 rails	10
	7½ ft	10 or 20 ft. long	60	4 rails	10
	8½ ft	10 or 20 ft. long	72	4 rails	10
Wooden posts and boards.	7½ ft.; 4 to 8 in	2 x 6 or 2 x 8 in. boards	60	4 boards	8
	8½ ft.; 4 to 8 in	2 x 6 or 2 x 8 in. boards	72	5 boards	8
Wooden posts and poles.	7½ ft.; 4 to 8 in	4 to 6 in. diameter	60	4 poles	8
	8½ ft.; 4 to 8 in	4 to 6 in. diameter	72	5 poles	8
Wooden posts and woven wire.	7½ ft.; 4 to 8 in	9 or 11 gage staywire	55 to 58	12-in. mesh	12

[1] Because of the strength of most metal, fewer rails and posts are necessary than when wood is used.

Horse Fences. Courtesy United States Department of Agriculture.

reason, that fine strand or two of electric wire certainly will not keep a horse confined. They have an uncanny ability of knowing when the current is off, and the careless owner may well find his horse out in the middle of his neighbor's front yard—or worse, out in the middle of the highway and involved in an accident.

A note of caution: electric wire should never be placed where a horse has to reach over it to eat or drink.

WHAT TO DO WITH MANURE

Every horse establishment, large or small, faces the problem of what to do with manure after it is removed from the stable. Fresh manure should never be spread on pastures being grazed by horses because it is a primary source of infestation by internal parasites. Some possible alternatives are as follows:

1. Spread fresh manure on fields that will be plowed and cropped.
2. Contact a nearby farmer or vegetable grower to remove the manure.
3. Store the manure in a tightly constructed pit for at least two weeks before spreading it. This allows the heat that is generated to destroy the parasites, their eggs, and their larvae.
4. Compost the manure where it will not pollute streams or ponds (or offend neighbors), and then spread it on the land.

5
Feeding the Horse

Beautiful, sleek horses are no accident. They are developed through careful breeding, good management, and proper feeding.

Feeding practices vary from locality to locality and handler to handler. They also vary depending on the purpose for which the horse is used, the size of the horse, the availability of feed, and the size of the equine establishment. However, a horse is basically a horse, and for this reason successful feeding in one stable usually is not much different from successful feeding in another stable.

TYPES OF FEED

Feeds can be classified into three main types:

1. Concentrates—the energy-rich grains, molasses, protein-and energy-rich supplements, vitamin and mineral supplements.
2. Roughages—pasture forages, hays, and silages.
3. Mixed feeds—commercially prepared in pellet form, these may be either high or low in energy, protein, or fiber, or they may provide a complete balanced ration.

CONCENTRATES

Oats, corn, barley, and milo (sorghum grain) are the most important energy-rich grains. They contain 70 to 80 percent TDN (total digestible nutrients), including 7 to 10 percent digestible protein. Wheat and rice bran, wheat or rye middlings, and rice polish are by-product feeds from the grain milling industry. The brans are bulky and laxative and contain about 65 percent TDN, of which up to 14 percent is digestible protein.

Among the protein supplements are soybean oil meal, cottonseed oil meal, and linseed oil meal. They average about 78 percent TDN and 40 percent digestible protein.

Mineral concentrates include salt, iodine, ground limestone, steamed bonemeal, and dicalcium phosphate. All of the vitamins can be obtained in concentrated form, in various combinations or singly.

The following feed formula (or variations of it) have been found to be successful by many horsepeople:

1100 pounds	Rolled oats
500 pounds	Cracked corn (you may wish to reduce this amount for summer feeding)
200 pounds	Soybean oil meal
100 pounds	Linseed oil meal
20 pounds	Trace mineral salt
20 pounds	Dicalcium phosphate
10 pounds	Calcium carbonate
1 pound	Vitamins A, D, and E
1 pound	Vitamin E
125 pounds	Wet molasses (or enough to eliminate dust in the feed)

For the stable with only a few horses, or when only small quantities of feed are required or little storage space is available, you may find it more satisfactory to buy ready-mixed feeds. There are many good ones available, but check the ingredients on the bag for nutrient value.

ROUGHAGE

There are three main forms of roughage:

1. Dry roughage—hay, straw, and artificially dehydrated forages (pellet form).
2. Silages—formed from green forages such as grass, alfalfa, sorghum, and corn, and preserved in a silo.
3. Pastures—green, growing grasses or legumes.

Generally speaking, the best hay for horses is a good quality grass-legume. Pure legume or pure grass hay is satisfactory if it is fed properly.

Grass hays such as timothy, oat, brome, bermuda, wheatgrass, and native western moutain grass, among others of equal quality, have similar nutrient values. (Prairie hay is much lower in protein than most other grass hays).

Legume hays such as alfalfa, soybean, peanut, lespedeza, and clovers are generally higher in protein, energy, calcium, and phosphorus than grass hays.

WHAT TO LOOK FOR IN GOOD HAY

Leafiness of the hay is an important guide to food value, because most of the nutrients are carried in the leaves. Horses refuse and waste more hay that is low in leaf content and stalky.

Odor of hay will vary with the type of legumes and grasses, but all hay should be aromatic and pleasant to smell. Lack of odor indicates old hay or overmaturity at the time of harvesting. This hay probably has lost most of its vitamin A value. Do not feed stale, musty, or moldy hay. It can be easily identified by a foul odor that indicates the hay was "put up" too wet and fermentation has occurred.

The color of the hay is another good indication of quality. Good hay is bright green. Overly mature hay is pale yellow or brown.

Dust is to be avoided in any feed for horses. It not only reduces the palatability of the feed, but also can cause heaves and other respiratory ailments. Pure legume hays tend to be more dusty than grass or mixed hay; timothy tends to be the most dust-free. To reduce dustiness in any feed, sprinkle it with water just before it is fed.

SILAGE

Quality silages can be a suitable replacement for up to half of the hay or pasture allowance. About 3 pounds of silage are equivalent to 1 pound of hay because of the difference in dry matter content. Never use spoiled, moldy, or frozen silages. These cause digestive upsets in horses, and silage that contains dead rats or birds can cause fatal botulism poisoning.

PASTURES

Pastures can greatly reduce feed costs and provide plenty of vitamins and proteins as well as exercise for the horse.

Horses should be rotated to fresh pasture every two or three weeks if possible. This will help reduce internal parasite infestation and increase the productivity of pastures, especially if they are small.

Pasture forages are laxative to the horse in early spring. Therefore, laxative feeds such as linseed oil meal or wheat bran should be removed from the grain ration when the horse first goes on pasture.

MIXED FEEDS

Some horsepeople are interested in complete, all-pelleted feed, in which the hay and grain are combined. (Pelleted feeds may be prepared from concentrates alone, forage alone, or concentrates and roughage combined in a complete ration). These concentrates do have some advantages insofar as they are less bulky and easier to store. Pelleting eliminates dustiness and lessens the likelihood of heaves, and pellet-fed horses may be trimmer in the middle because they consume less bulk.

While most horsepeople acknowledge that all-pellet feeding virtually eliminates waste, many persist in the feeling that the horse, particularly one that spends most of the time in a stall, needs "nibbling" food and that the pelleted rations are more likely to cause wood-chewing than regular grain and long hay.

WATER

It is best for the horse if he has free access to clean, fresh, cool water. He will drink 10 to 12 gallons daily, depending on the weather, the amount of work required of him, and the rations he is fed. If free access to water is not possible, then the horse should be watered at approximately the same times daily and as frequently as possible. Water may be given before, during, or after feeding.

Do not allow a horse to drink heavily when he is hot. He may founder or colic. Do not allow a horse to drink heavily just before being put to work. Clean the water container frequently, particularly during warm weather.

The digestive tract of a horse is quite small considering the size of the animal. Compared to that of a cow, it is considerably smaller. Therefore, it is more economical to feed the horse smaller amounts at more frequent intervals than it is to feed him a large amount at one time.

HORSE

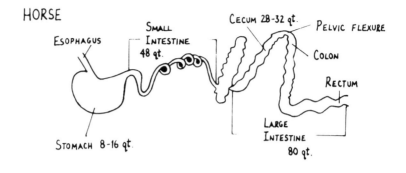

COW

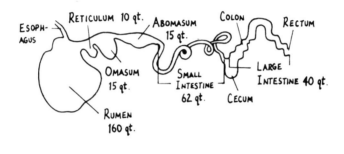

PIG

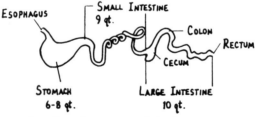

Comparative digestive tracts of the horse, cow, and pig.

The grain ration is usually divided into three equal feedings given morning, noon, and night. A good practice for feeding hay is to feed one-fourth of the daily hay allowance at each the morning and noon feedings and the remaining one-half at night when the animal has plenty of time to eat at his leisure.

Just like their human counterparts, horses learn to anticipate their feed. Therefore, they should be fed at the same time each day.

Avoid sudden changes in diet, especially when changing from a less concentrated ration to a richer one. When ingredients are added or omitted, the change should be made gradually. A sudden change can cause digestive disturbances, make the horse to "go off" his feed, or result in colic or even founder. This same caution should be exercised in turning horses to pasture or in transferring them to more lush grazing. A horse that has been on dry feed should be turned to pasture for no more than two hours the first day. The time may be increased to two to three hours the second day and three to four hours the third day. By gradually increasing the length of time, at the end of a week the horse will be on full pasture forage with no problems.

Unfortunately, little experimental work has been done on the minimum nutritional requirements of horses. However, available information from the United States Department of Agriculture, shown in the tables will meet the minimum requirements for horses and provide a reasonable margin of safety.

The classical horse ration of grass, grass hay, and farm grains is usually deficient in calcium but adequate in phosphorus. This ration almost always is deficient in salt and usually iodine. Thus horses nearly always need mineral supplements. Salt, calcium, and phosphorus requirements not met by feeds can best be supplied by allowing the horse free access to a salt-mineral block.

High-quality, leafy, green forages plus plenty of sunshine generally give horses most of the vitamins they need. Horses get carotene (which they convert into vitamin A) and riboflavin from green pasture and

—Recommended allowances of protein, fiber, and total digestible nutrients (TDN)

Type of horse	Minimum crude protein	Maximum crude fiber	Minimum TDN
	Percent	*Percent*	*Percent*
Most mature horses used for race, show, or pleasure _____	12	25	[1] 53 to 70
Broodmares _____	13	25	50 to 60
Stallions _____	14	25	[2] 50 to 68
Young equines:			
Foals, 2 weeks to 10 months old _____	21	8	68 to 74
Weanlings to 18 months old _____	14	20	60
18 months to 3 years old _____	13	25	50 to 60

[1] The heavier the work, the more energy is required.
[2] Increase the energy immediately before and during the breeding season.

Recommended allowances of protein, fiber, and total digestible nutrients (TDN). Courtesy U.S. Department of Agriculture.

Kind of mineral or vitamin	Daily allowance per 1,000-pound horse [1]	Allowance per ton of finished feed (hay and grain combined) [2]
Minerals:		
Salt	2 oz.	10 lb.
Calcium	70.0 g.	12.33 lb.
Phosphorus	60.0 g.	10.57 lb.
Magnesium	3,200 mg.	256 g.
Iron	640 mg.	51.2 g.
Zinc	400 mg.	32.0 g.
Manganese	340 mg.	27.2 g.
Copper	90 mg.	7.2 g.
Iodine	2.6 mg.	.21 g.
Cobalt	1.5 mg.	.12 g.
Vitamins:		
Vitamin A _____USP__	50,000	4,000,000
Vitamin D₂ _____USP__	7,000	560,000
Vitamin E _____IU__	200	16,000
Choline _____mg__	400	32,000
Pantothenic acid__mg__	60	4,800
Niacin _____mg__	50	4,000
Riboflavin _____mg__	40	3,200
Thiamine (B₁) ___mg__	25	2,000
Vitamin K _____mg__	8	640
Folic acid _____mg__	2.5	200
Vitamin B₁₂ _____μg [3]__	125	10,000

[1] This is based on an allowance of 25 pounds of feed per 1,000-pound horse per day, or 2.5 pounds of feed per 100 pounds of body weight.

[2] Where hay is fed separately, double this amount should be added to the concentrate.

[3] Micrograms.

Recommended allowances of minerals and vitamins. Courtesy U.S. Department of Agriculture.

green hay not over a year old. Horses get vitamin D from sunlight and sun-cured hay.

AMOUNT TO FEED

How much to feed a horse is a matter as individual as each horse. It is not at all unusual for two horses of the same breed living in the same barn, doing the same amount of work, to require widely varying amounts of food. In other words, some horses are easy keepers and some are hard keepers.

The table giving the feeding guide for light horses suggests quantities to feed. However, it is intended only as a guide. The best proof of proper feeding is demonstrated by the health, condition, and stamina of the individual horse.

Because of the limited digestive capacity of the horse, the amount of

—Light horse feeding guide

Age, sex, and use	Daily allowance	Kind of hay	Suggested grain rations		
			Rations No. 1	Rations No. 2	Rations No. 3
			Pounds	*Pounds*	*Pounds*
Stallions in breeding season (weighing 900 to 1,400 lb.).	¾ to 1½ lb. grain per 100 lb. body weight, together with a quantity of hay within same range.	Grass-legume mixed; or ⅓ to ½ legume hay, with remainder grass hay.	Oats 55 Wheat 20 Wheat bran 20 Linseed meal 5	Corn 35 Oats 35 Wheat 15 Wheat bran 15	Oats 100
Pregnant mares (weighing 900 to 1,400 lb.).	¾ to 1½ lb. grain per 100 lb. body weight, together with a quantity of hay within same range.	Grass-legume mixed; or ⅓ to ½ legume hay, with remainder grass hay (straight grass hay may be used first half of pregnancy).	Oats 80 Wheat bran 20	Barley 45 Oats 45 Wheat bran 10	Oats 95 Linseed meal 5
Foals before weaning (weighing 100 to 350 lb. with projected mature weights of 900 to 1,400 lb.).	½ to ¾ lb. grain per 100 lb. body weight, together with a quantity of hay within same range.	Legume hay	Oats 50 Wheat bran 40 Linseed meal 10 Rations balanced on basis of following assumption: Mares of mature weights of 600, 800, 1,000, and 1,200 lb. may produce 36, 42, 44, and 49 lb. of milk daily.	Oats 30 Barley 30 Wheat bran 30 Linseed meal 10	Oats 80 Wheat bran 20
Weanlings (weighing 350 to 450 lb.).	1 to 1½ lb. grain and 1½ to 2 lb. hay per 100 lb. body weight.	Grass-legume mixed; or ½ legume hay, with remainder grass hay.	Oats 30 Barley 30 Wheat bran 30 Linseed meal 10	Oats 70 Wheat bran 15 Linseed meal 15	Oats 80 Linseed meal 20
Yearlings, 2d summer (weighing 450 to 700 lb.).	Good, luxuriant pasture (if in training or for other reasons without access to pasture, the ration should be intermediate between the adjacent upper and lower groups).				
Yearlings, or rising 2-year-olds, second winter (weighing 700 to 1,000 lb.).	½ to 1 lb. grain and 1 to 1½ lb. hay per 100 lb. body weight.	Grass-legume mixed; or ⅓ to ½ legume hay, with remainder grass hay.	Oats 80 Wheat bran 20	Barley 35 Oats 35 Bran 15 Linseed meal 15	Oats 100
Light horses at work; riding, driving, and racing (weighing 900 to 1,400 lb.).	Hard use—1¼ to 1⅓ lb. grain and 1 to 1¼ lb. hay per 100 lb. body weight. Medium use—¾ to 1 lb. grain and 1 to 1¼ lb. hay per 100 lb. body weight. Light use—⅖ to ½ lb. grain and 1¼ to 1½ lb. hay per 100 lb. body weight.	Grass hay	Oats 100	Oats 70 Corn 30	Oats 70 Barley 30
Mature idle horses; stallions, mares, and geldings (weighing 900 to 1,400 lb.).	1½ to 1¾ lb. hay per 100 lb. body weight.	Pasture in season; or grass-legume mixed hay.	(With grass hay, add ¾ lb. of a high protein supplement daily.)		

Note.—With all rations and for all classes and ages of horses, provide free access to separate containers of (1) iodized salt and (2) a mixture of 1 part salt and 2 parts steamed bonemeal or other suitable calcium-phosphorous supplement.

Feeding guide for light horses. Courtesy U. S. Department of Agriculture.

concentrates (grains) must be increased and the roughages (hay) decreased when the energy needs rise with more work: horses at light work, one to three hours per day of riding or driving; horses at medium work, three to five hours per day of riding or driving; and horses at hard work, five to eight hours per day of riding or driving.

With all rations and for all classes and ages of horses, provide free access to separate containers of (1) iodized salt and (2) a mixture of one part salt and two parts steamed bonemeal or other suitable calcium-phosphorous or salt-mineral block.

GENERAL FEEDING RULES

1. Do not feed an extremely fatigued horse a full feed.
2. Do not work the animal immediately after a full feed.
3. If you plan to work a horse hard after feeding, feed him only half ration. Feed him the other half later.
4. Do not feed grain to a hot animal. Hay will not harm him.
5. If the horse has a tendency to throw feed out of his grain box, place a smooth rock on it.
6. Feed whole, cracked, or crimped grain. Grain that has been *ground* is too fine in texture and can cause impaction in the digestive tract.
7. Never give dirty, moldy, musty, dusty, or frozen feed.
8. Keep the feed and water containers clean.
9. Inspect the feed box regularly to see if the horse goes off his feed. Horses love to eat. If he isn't eating, there is a reason. Consult your veterinarian.
10. If a horse slobbers, tips his head to one side, or otherwise indicates difficulty in eating, he may be having some problem with his teeth. Consult your veterinarian.
11. Rope hay nets are useful if mangers are not available.
12. If the horse's manure becomes hard and dry, give him occasional bran mash. Green grass also is an excellent laxative.
13. The horse should have green grass whenever it is available, even if you have to stand with him and let him eat in the front yard. Never tie him to a tree or stake and leave him unattended.
14. Clean water and salt should be available to the horse at all times.
15. Colic can be the result of a drastic change in the horse's diet. Don't fool around with colic. Call the veterinarian immediately.
16. The horse will delight in having a treat occasionally. Carrots or apples seem to be a favorite, although many horses are fond of citrus fruits and a great variety of other foods. Avoid fruits with pits, such as cherries or plums, unless the pit is first removed.

PASTURE POISONING

Horses pasturing on Sudan grass or a sorghum-Sudan grass hybrid must be removed from this pasture at first frost. Frost causes prussic acid to form in the plant, which can be, and usually is, fatal to horses.

Johnson grass or other sorghums raised in subtropical regions are capable of producing hydrocyanic poison if they have suffered stunting caused by dry weather or faulty irrigation. Do not turn a horse on such a pasture. The same caution is applied to sweet clover in excessively dry years.

POISON PLANTS

It would be impossible to list all the plants that are poisonous to horses, but a few of the common ones are Bracken fern, privet, ragwort, vetch, yew, oak leaves and acorns, colchicum (meadow saffron), cocklebur (first leaves and seedlings), horsetail, and loco weed.

As a general rule, horses will not eat poisonous plants when there is plenty of other food available. However, cases of poisoning can occur through poisonous plants being included in the hay at hay-making time. Treatment of poisoned animals is usually futile, so the best approach is prevention. First identify the poisonous plants in your area; second, prevent access; and third, get rid of the plants wherever possible.

6
Grooming

A well-groomed horse usually indicates a well-cared for horse. It shows you care, and it's a point of pride in ownership. Regular grooming helps maintain health and condition. It cleans the hair, keeps the skin functioning naturally, minimizes skin disease and parasites, and improves the condition and fitness of muscles. It also affords the opportunity to thoroughly inspect the horse's body for any skin problems that may be developing or for lacerations or cuts he may have gotten in the stall or pasture.

Horsepeople have always accepted the fact that the horse enjoys being groomed, so it is an excellent way to gain rapport with your horse, to really get to know him. As always, when working around the horse, work quietly. You will be rewarded by gaining his confidence.

The essential tools needed for grooming are as follows:

Rubber curry comb
Body brush
Hoof pick
Sweat scraper
Rub rags (old turkish towels are excellent)

Optional equipment includes:

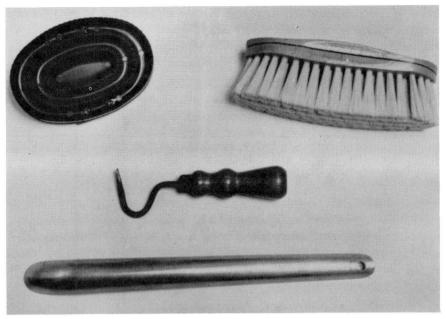

Grooming Tools. Top left—*rubber curry comb.* Top right—*brush.* Center—*hoof pick.* Lower—*sweat scraper.*

Dandy brush
Mane brush (a human hair brush is fine)

It is convenient to have a box of sufficient size to hold the grooming tools. This can be fitted with a strap handle across the top for easy carrying. If you don't have a box, or can't make one, an ordinary bucket will hold your tools nicely. Either box or bucket may be kept in the tack room or some other out-of-the-way place and taken to the cross ties or stall where the horse is to be cleaned. It is also best that each horse have separate grooming equipment. This is for the protection of all the horses in the barn. Skin diseases are easily spread by shared grooming tools.

GROOMING PROCEDURE AND METHOD

Grooming with the curry comb should start at the neck, where it enters the head, and continue toward the rear, finishing at the hocks. The curry comb is never used on the lower legs. Use the curry comb in a rotary motion to loosen dust and scurf. Proceed in the following order: neck, breast, withers, shoulders, foreleg (only as far down as the knee), back, side, belly, croup, and hind leg down to the hock. During the process the dirt accumulated in the curry comb should be removed frequently by tapping it against the wall or some other hard object.

The brush should then be used with the grain of the hair, again starting at the neck and ending at the hocks. The brush can be used on the lower parts of the legs if they are excessively dirty or mud caked. The general rule on grooming is "curry gently, brush vigorously." During grooming the brush should be cleaned frequently by pulling it against the tooth edges of the curry comb.

Follow the brushing with the rub rag. It should be used over the entire body as well as on the head, ears, lips, legs, and back of the pasterns. Finally, wipe out the nostrils, dock, and underparts of the tail with a damp cloth or sponge.

There's nothing like the human hand for that added bit of sheen. For the extra special grooming job, use your hand as you would the final rub rug.

Worthy of note is the fact that some mares, when in season, may become sensitive on the flank and other rear areas. The wise horseperson will be aware of this and groom gently.

If a beautiful mane and tail are desired, great care should be taken in their grooming. Just as the crowning glory of a beautiful person is the hair, the crowning glory of a beautiful horse is the mane and tail. Usually show horses never have a brush laid to the mane and tail. Instead they are worked out, hair by hair, with the fingers. However, if you prefer to use the mane brush, use it judiciously, because if it is not carefully handled, it will pull out the hair.

After the body has been cleaned, each foot should be lifted and picked out. Use a hoof pick (or an old screwdriver can make an adequate tool), and work from the heel to the toe. Be sure to clean the depressions between the frog and the bars thoroughly. Daily cleaning will go a long way in preventing thrush or hoof rot.

While cleaning the hoof also inspect for cracks and loose shoes or dryness of the hoof. If the hoof is dry, apply a liberal coating of hoof dressing (see Chapter 9).

Grooming equipment should be washed at intervals to be kept clean. Use warm water and soap; then disinfect as a precaution against skin diseases.

There is no place in a good barn for a metal curry comb with teeth. These harsh tools can severely irritate and scratch a horse's sensitive skin, leaving him readily subject to skin disease—to say nothing of making him sore when a saddle is placed on his back.

TRIMMING

To make the horse more attractive and to prevent the mane from bunching up when the bridle is in position, it is customary to trim a bridle path. This is done by simply trimming a 6-inch path of mane in the area immediately behind the poll. This can be done with a pair of scissors or an electric clipper.

If you show your horse, the trimming preparation for the show ring will be more extensive. This is done to show off the horse to his best advantage. In addition to the bridle path, the whiskers and any long hair that may be on the cheek, jaw, or throat latch are trimmed. The ears, both inside and around the rim, are clipped.

Fetlock hair and hair that falls over the coronet band, and any shaggy hairs that may grow randomly on the legs should be trimmed. This trimming can be accomplished with careful use of scissors; however, an electric clipper is definitely an asset. Care should be used to avoid notching the hair. A wad of cotton may be placed in the horse's ears to reduce some of the clipper noise and to prevent hair from falling in his ears.

Keep in mind that once the hair has been clipped from inside the horse's ear he has lost his natural protection. Nature put that fine hair there to keep insects out of the delicate inner ear. Therefore, to turn the horse back out to pasture without this defense would be cruel and could well prove damaging to him. It is wise to keep the horse inside until the hair has grown back. If the horse must be put outside, put an ear net on him. For a nominal price an ear net can be purchased from your tack shop or supply catalog.

Also remember that the fetlock hair is no longer there to divert water from the tender area of the heel. When you tamper with nature's careful work, it becomes your responsibility to see that the horse is not left on his own to suffer the consequences.

BATHING

If regularly and properly groomed, the horse usually will not need a bath. However, many owners who compete in the show ring prefer to bathe their horses in preparation for competition.

There are two cautions about bathing: (1) never bathe the horse in cold weather unless you have a heated area in which to work and keep the horse until he is completely dry, and (2) use extreme care in removing all traces of shampoo.

For bathing, always use *warm* water and a mild shampoo. Detergents are drying to the skin and hair and can be an irritant. There are many commercial horse shampoos available on the market. However, mild human shampoo is just as serviceable and usually less expensive.

For the bath, make a sudsy solution of shampoo and warm water in a bucket. A large sponge makes a good washcloth. Start at the neck behind the ears and work in the same manner as if you were grooming, all the time keeping the sponge well filled with the sudsy solution. Do not use soap or shampoo on the head and ears! A damp clean cloth will do a fine job on these areas.

After the horse is completely soaped, with extra attention given to such things as white stockings, rinse him thoroughly with warm water. Be sure all traces of shampoo have been rinsed completely from the horse's hair and skin.

When the rinsing is complete, use the sweat scraper to remove excess water, and then rub the horse dry with clean towels or rub rags. Keep him out of drafts until he is completely dry. If the weather is the least bit cool, cover him with a blanket or cooler. The cooler will not only guard against the chill, it will also help lay the hair flat.

INSECT CONTROL

In warm weather insects are natural tormentors of the horse, and he cannot escape them. Some relief can be offered by the use of insect repellents, and there are many good commercial products on the market, both sprays and wipes. A note of caution, however: do not use stable or barn spray on the horse. The chance is almost 100 percent that it will burn his skin. Stable or barn spray is for use in and on the stable or barn.

Also avoid getting any spray in the horse's water or feed. Use a product designed specifically for use on the horse. Even with these products you frequently run into problems of burning the skin or allergic reactions, so always make a patch test on a small area and be certain there is no adverse reaction before you spray or wipe his entire body.

Exercise caution in the use of repellents, and do not get any in the horse's eyes. If you should inadvertently get some in the eyes, flush the area immediately with plenty of clean warm water.

7
Exercising Your Horse

To keep your horse in top condition, feeling and doing his best, he must have regular exercise. It is grossly unfair, even cruel, to leave a horse standing in a box stall without exercise, sunshine, or fresh air for days or weeks on end. It could be likened to someone locking you in a closet and expecting you to thrive. Without exercise a horse rapidly loses muscle tone and is likely to pick up bad stall habits, such as wood chewing, weaving, or kicking, from sheer boredom.

You can exercise your horse in the following ways:

1. Allowing him access to paddock or pasture where he can exercise himself.
2. Riding or driving.
3. Lunging.

Invariably the novice horse owner will ask, "How long should I ride or exercise my horse?" Depending on how many people he asks, he will receive answers all the way from "no longer than twenty minutes" to "at least five hours, and work the tar out of him."

Your own common sense must prevail. The reasonable answer to that question will depend on just what kind of exercise you've got in mind. You could not reasonably expect a person who sits behind a desk forty hours a week and whose primary source of exercise is walking to and from the dinner table to go out to the country and run for five hours. Neither should you expect heavy work from a horse who is subject to very limited exercise. He simply is not in condition. Your horse must be conditioned for the kind of work you expect him to do.

PADDOCK OR PASTURE EXERCISE

If you are not able to ride, drive, or lunge your horse on a reasonably regular basis, it is almost a necessity to give him access to a paddock or pasture where he can exercise himself freely. This sort of exercise not only provides the opportunity for him to "limber up" and keep in reasonable condition, it affords him access to sunlight and fresh air.

RIDING OR DRIVING

When riding or driving a horse that has been confined to his stall for several days, *walk* him for the first mile and then let him jog a bit before you urge him to do any strenuous work. Give him time to loosen his muscles and joints.

When completing your ride, allow him to walk the last mile, or long enough to cool off, before you return him to his stall. If he is not cooled by the time you are ready to put him up, follow the "cooling" procedure.

COOLING

Spring or summer, winter or fall, and regardless of climate, *always* cool out a "hot" horse. A hot horse is one that has been worked hard enough to become lathered with sweat and to breathe hard, at a rapid rate. The term "cooling out" is applied to the process of slowing down the rate at which the horse's body returns to its normal functions. If a horse cools out too fast, the results can be dire.

First, get the horse out of any drafts and remove his tack. In this case, the care of the horse definitely takes precedence over the cleaning of the equipment. Remove excess perspiration with the sweat scraper, and rub him down briskly and well with towels. If the weather is cool put a sheet or cooler on the animal.

Use common sense here. If the temperature is 95 degrees, don't throw a pile of wool coolers on the horse and confine him in a stagnant pocket of air. The idea is to cool him out, not give him a heat stroke.

Walk the horse slowly, in a relaxed manner, until his breathing rate has returned to normal and he has stopped sweating.

If you have ever participated in vigorous athletic sports or exercise, you are aware of the fact that your body rapidly becomes dehydrated. Common sense tells you that the same thing happens to the horse's body after strenuous work. Therefore, he needs water to aid him in his cooling process. However, only offer him small amounts at one time. Under no circumstances allow him to consume large quantities of cold water. This could produce such a shock to his "hot" system that it could cause colic.

A hot horse should *never* be fed grain. This could also cause colic or founder. He may, however, be fed some hay.

LUNGING

The lunge line is a strap, web, or rope some 25 feet in length, which the handler uses by standing approximately in one spot while the horse moves in a circle around him.

For lunging you will need the following:

1. A strap, web, or rope some 20-25 feet in length. (A light, strong, cotton rope is excellent).
2. A lunge whip or a long whip with a lash at the end.
3. A halter of serviceable weight (or you may wish to purchase a lunging halter).

Snap the lunge line to the ring of the chin strap of the halter (if using a lunging halter use the dee-ring). Lead the horse to the center of an enclosure approximately 50 feet square. Hold the lunge line in your left hand, and show him the lash whip, which is held in your right hand. Generally the horse will immediately move away at the sight of the whip toward one side of the enclosure.

Depending on his age, spirit, and condition, he may plunge away, canter, or buck. This makes no difference. Let him have his fun. He will soon get the kinks out of himself and settle down. After a round or two, he may stop. If he does, lay the whiplash to the ground at his rear, and he will start again. If he turns in the center to come toward you, show him the whip, and he will head back toward the side of the enclosure.

In starting the horse on the lunge line be sure that you are to the rear of his line of vision and not in front of it. The sight of you in front of him will tend to make him stop. When not actively using your lunge whip to direct the horse, you should keep the lash end trailing on the

Lunging the horse.

ground behind you, away from the horse. If he catches sight of it in front of him, he will be inclined to stop.

To change direction, stop the horse. Encourage him with your voice and a gentle tug on the line to walk toward you. Reward him with a pat on the shoulder. Then reverse your lunge line and whip with the lunge line in your right hand and the lash whip in your left. Repeat the procedure.

The amount of time spent in lunging the horse will vary with the individual, his age, condition, temperament, and training. But on the average twenty minutes of lunging a day will provide adequate exercise.

With patient, intelligent handling, and prudent use of the lunge whip, you can train your horse to voice commands (whoa, walk, trot, and canter) in a short period of time. Any whip, including the lunge whip, should be considered and used only as an extension of the handler's (or rider's) arm. It is a tool to aid you in training and directing your horse and should not be used as an instrument with which to beat your animal. Only the most ignorant of people resort to beating their horses, and then it serves no useful purpose. It only produces resentment and fear on the part of the horse.

It also goes without saying that if the horse has become heated while lunging, he must be cooled out before being returned to his stall.

Rough treatment on a lunge line may cause abrupt turns and throw a horse off balance. This is especially true with a young horse and could be the cause of injuries such as splints, curbs, cuts, or bruises. Such injury can be partially guarded against by the use of shin boots. However, the best protection is a wise handler on the center end of the lunge line.

8
Trailering the Horse

Horses are transported from one point to another by trailer, van, truck, train, boat, or airplane. But far and away most horses are hauled in a one or two horse trailer drawn behind a truck or car. By whatever means a horse is to be moved from one place to another, the prime consideration must be to move him safely.

A horse is a large, heavy animal. Therefore the vehicle in which the horse is to be moved must be of sturdy construction with a solid, strong floor. More than one hapless animal has been placed in a trailer with a rotten floor and has wound up with the floor breaking beneath him, his legs dragging along the pavement, while the ignoramus driver is merrily speeding his way down the highway.

Assuming that the floor of the vehicle is sound and sturdy, in order to provide good footing for the horse it should be lined with heavy coco matting, rubber mats, or sand covered with straw or other suitable bedding material. If the transit is to be a long one, clean the floor covering at frequent intervals to avoid the buildup of ammonia and heat.

When hauling with a horse trailer, you should make certain the hitch is in good order, properly attached, and secured. Check the lights and brakes to see that they are functioning properly before you start.

The need to drive carefully cannot be stressed too strongly. Drive at a moderate, constant speed as opposed to fast or jerky driving. Accelerate slowly and steadily from a stop, reduce speed on curves, and turn corners with care. A sure way to make a horse "trailer shy," to say nothing of actually doing him injury, is giving him a rough ride. Stay constantly alert to what is happening on the road in front of you. Leave sufficient distance between yourself and the vehicle ahead to make a safe stop if necessary. The last thing you want to do is slam on your brakes.

An excellent way to find out just what it feels like in that trailer when it is moving is to get in it yourself and have someone take you for a little ride (minus the horse, of course). This will quickly give you an idea of what you should and should not do as a driver.

WHEN TRANSPORTING HORSES

Feed lightly. Allow the horse only a half ration of grain before shipment and a half ration for the first feed after he has reached his destination. While in transit give him all the good quality hay he will eat (preferably alfalfa to help keep his bowels moving), but no grain should be fed.

Some vehicles are equipped with a built-in place for the hay. If yours does not have this, use commercial rope nets or homemade burlap containers to hold the hay. Care should be taken that the hay nets are not placed so high that the horse has trouble eating from them or so low that he can get a leg caught in them.

Water liberally. When transporting, you should give the horse all the fresh clean water he will drink at frequent intervals. If the weather is extremely hot, avoid offering cold water because there is danger of the horse gorging himself. A case of colic while in transit is the last thing you, or the horse, need. To avoid taste change in water and the possibility of the horse refusing it, add a small amount of molasses to his water beginning about a week before he is to be shipped.

Ventilate adequately. Provide plenty of fresh air without drafts. In cold weather the horse may be blanketed. However, care should be taken to see that he does not get tangled in it.

Have the horse relaxed and rested. Horses ship best if they are not overtired and tense before they are moved. A nervous, excitable horse or one known to be a "bad hauler" may be calmed by a tranquilizer. This should be administered by a veterinarian prior to loading the horse.

Pad the stalls. Most experienced shippers prefer padding inside the vehicle to lessen the likelihood of injury. Also check carefully for any protruding nails or other hazards that might cause injury.

Take company. If at all possible, avoid hauling horses alone. If you have a flat tire, engine problems, or the horse gets in trouble, it is more than likely that you are going to need help.

Carry tools and equipment. In case of emergency you should have ready access to the following equipment: a pinch bar, a hammer, a hatchet, a saw, nails, pliers, a flashlight, an extra halter and shanks, gloves, a fork and a broom. For an extended haul it is a good idea to have medication for colic and shipping fever provided by a veterinarian.

Control insects. In season, flies and other insects molest animals in transit. Use a reliable insecticide to control insects. Follow directions on the container label.

Tying the horse in the vehicle. Use a 5/8-inch cotton rope shank that is 5 feet long and has a big swivel snap at the end. Tie with a knot that can easily and quickly be released in case of emergency. *When tying the horse in the trailer or van, do not run a chain shank over his nose or under his chin.* Allow enough slack in the rope for the horse to get at his hay comfortably, but not enough for him to turn his head to the side or strike it on the top of the vehicle. A shipping rope snapped around the horse's neck and secured to a dee-ring at the side is an added precaution.

Avoid shoes. Whenever possible, ship horses barefoot. Do not allow them to wear calked shoes on a long shipment. They are not only hard on the horse's legs, but can get caught in the mats or padding.

Bandage the legs. Legs should be bandaged to keep the ankles from getting scuffed, the coronet damaged, or the tendons bruised. This is especially desirable for show horses, race horses, or valuable breeding stock. A horse should not be shipped in leg bandages, however, until he is familiar with the feel and is comfortable in wearing them. Practice wrapping the legs several times, and allow the horse to become familiar with them before you ship.

To bandage the legs you will need the following:

1. Cotton, cotton sheets, or quilted padding
2. Bandages of knit jersey or flannel

Apply a thick layer of cotton or quilted padding around the horse's leg. Make sure it is placed low enough to adequately cover and protect the coronet. The bandage itself is started on the cannon bone just above the ankle. It is rolled flatly and firmly down to catch securely under the ankle, and then back up the leg, ending just below the knee.

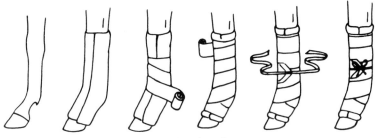

Shipping bandages.

Fasten with a large safety pin or tie with the strings attached to the end of the bandage. The bandage is rolled tightly enough to keep it from slipping down, but not so tight as to hinder circulation of blood in the legs. This same caution must be applied to tying the strings.

Be calm when loading and unloading. When loading and unloading horses, always be patient and never demonstrate anger. Try kindness first; pat the horse, speak to him, and reassure him. Even a little bribery with a handful of oats or a bit of carrot may be useful. If this fails, it may be necessary to use more forceful methods to get the horse loaded. However, for the neophite horse-owner, if more forceful methods are required, it is best to seek an experienced "loader" for assistance.

Clean and disinfect a public conveyance. Before using any type of rented or public conveyance, always thoroughly clean and disinfect it. Check carefully for nails or other hazards that might cause injury. Also inspect it thoroughly to be sure it is a safe vehicle in which to haul your horse.

Have a health certificate and proof of ownership. A health certificate signed by a licensed veterinarian is required for most interstate shipments. Transport across foreign borders must be accompanied by a health certificate and negative Coggins test that has been approved by a government veterinarian. This may take several days. Branded horses must be accompanied by a brand certificate, and all transporters should have a statement of ownership.

9
Shoeing the Horse

The old axiom "no feet, no horse" has been around for hundreds of years, and it is just as true today as it was the first time it was voiced. The legs and feet are the most vulnerable parts of the horse. Therefore they should be subject to scrupulous care, because the value of a horse lies chiefly in his ability to move.

One of the prime factors in the care of the horse's feet are the services of a competent farrier. Horseshoeing is a specialized art as well as a skilled craft. Such technical work is best kept out of the hands of the untrained and left to the expert.

One such expert is Gil Reaume of Williamston, Michigan. Reaume has many years experience in the shoeing of draft horses, American Saddle Horses, Hackneys, Morgans, Arabians, Standardbreds, speed and action horses, hunters, and jumpers. He specializes in hand-made shoes, quarter crack repair, and the correction of faulty gaits.

The following questions asked by novice horsepeople were posed to Reaume:

Q. What is the most important thing I should do in caring for my horse's feet?
A. There are but three things: (1) keep them clean, (2) prevent them

from drying out, and (3) keep them trimmed so they retain their proper shape and length.

Q. Why is hoof care so important?

A. The value of a horse depends on his ability to work, be it racing, showing, pulling, or simply taking his owner for a nice ride down the road. To this end, four sound feet are absolutely necessary.

Q. Horses in the wild do not have shoes or a farrier to take care of their feet. Why is it so important for my horse?

A. Wild horses seem to have been practically free from serious foot trouble. Predators generally made short work of those who weren't, which eliminated the perpetuation of weak-footed animals through breeding. But when horses were domesticated, the troubles we see today began to appear.

The horse was brought from soft pasture to hard roads, from self-regulated exercise to rigorous work demanded of him by his owner, from healthy pasture to filthy housing where he was often made to stand in his own feces and urine or mud, and from a light maintenance diet of natural grasses to the heavy, artificial ration necessary for the work required of him. Even the basically sound horse frequently breaks down under the harsh demands made upon him by humans and their misguided "care."

Q. Why does a horse's foot have to be trimmed?

A. The horse's hoof is much like your fingernails. It grows continuously, normally at the rate of 1/4 to 1/2 inch a month. The hoof wall grows out perpendicularly to the coronary band, so if the hoof is not worn off evenly this transfers excessive strain to flexor tendons. If the horse is shod and wears the same shoes too long, his base of support actually grows out from under him. If the shoes are worn too thin and become too loose or twisted, they can cause corns.

Q. How often does the hoof have to be trimmed or shod?

A. That depends on the rate of growth of the horse's foot, but generally it is every six to eight weeks. It's the same for trimming or resetting the shoes.

Q. Why do horses need shoes?

A. Shoes protect the hoof against excessive wear when hard or unusual work is required. They provide better traction under unfavorable conditions, such as walking on ice and mud. They help correct defects of stance or gait, often making it possible for an unsound horse to give satisfactory service. Shoes also may be used to help cure diseases or defects of the hoof, such as contracted heels, cracks in the hoof wall, bruised soles, or tendonitis. Shoes should always be made to fit the horse's feet, not the feet to fit the shoes.

Q. Do all horses need to be shod?

A. No. It is not necessary to shoe horses that are not being used hard enough to cause excessive wear or soreness to their feet or to correct a faulty way of moving. In such cases keeping the hoof trimmed at the proper angle is all that is necessary. Put it this way: there should be a reason to shoe a horse; don't shoe him simply as a routine procedure.

Q. What is the proper angle of a horse's foot?

A. That depends on the conformation of the horse. Generally the angle is somewhere between 50 and 55 degrees for the front feet and 53 to 57 degrees for the hind feet. Knowledge of the foot and leg is helpful in understanding foot care. The important thing to keep in mind is that the angle of the hoof should be the same as the angle of the pastern. If either the heel or the toe is too long, it will place strain unnaturally on the bones and tendons of the horse's foot and leg.

Q. What is a healthy foot?

A. A healthy foot is one that is free of thrush or disease. It is not dry and brittle, but supple enough to expand and contract when the horse moves on it (this helps the blood circulation in the foot). The healthy foot has the frog down near the ground, where there can be frog pressure to help pump this blood.

A healthy foot is also free of serious cracks. Some small cracks on the outside layer of the hoof wall are more a cosmetic problem than harmful. This is especially true in the unshod horse. As the hoof gets a little long, the outer layer of wall may chip   f and small cracks may form. These are of little consequence. The healthy foot also should have the periople intact.

Q. What is periople?

A. The periople is a thin, varnish-like outer layer of the hoof that nature provided as a protective coating to prevent evaporation of the hoof's moisture. Because this layer is so important in keeping a healthy foot, it is wise not to rasp the walls of the hoof.

Q. What is thrush?

A. Thrush is a disease affecting the cleft of the frog. It is characterized by a foul odor accompanied by a blackish moisture or oozing. It softens and decays the tissues in the cleft of the frog or in the junction between the frog and the bars. This disease is usually associated with improper cleaning of the horse's hoof and dirty, wet barn conditions.

Thrush can be treated readily in its early stages by cleaning the foot thoroughly. Loose and ragged pieces of frog should be pared away to allow a good approach to the site of the trouble. Cotton should then be carefully packed into the crevices of the foot, and a liberal dressing of thrush medication should be applied.

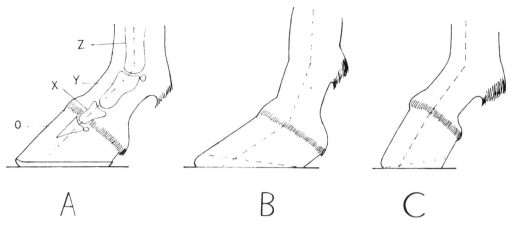

A. Properly trimmed hoof showing normal foot axis. Z, cannon bone; Y, long pastern bone; X, short pastern bone; O, coffin bone.
B. Foot axis breaks backward because the toe is too long. The horizontal dotted line indicates how the hoof should be trimmed to effect correct posture.
C. The foot axis breaks forward because the heel is too long. The horizontal dotted line indicates how the hoof should be trimmed to effect normal posture.

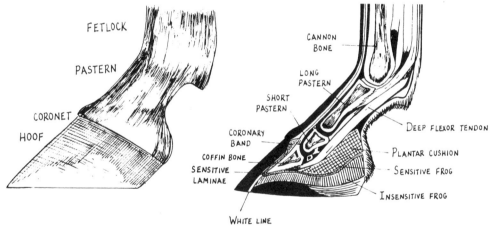

Parts of the horse's foot.

One or two such treatments will usually clear up a mild case of thrush. However, if you don't take measures to correct the conditions that caused the thrush in the first place, the horse will certainly get it again. If the case of thrush is advanced or if there is pain involved, you should contact your veterinarian for more specific treatment.

Q. What can be done for dry or brittle feet?

A. Dry, brittle feet are a problem especially in the arid regions of the country. This condition usually can be prevented by keeping the ground wet around the watering tank. It can be relieved by packing the feet with wet clay, or other commercial compounds, once or twice a week.

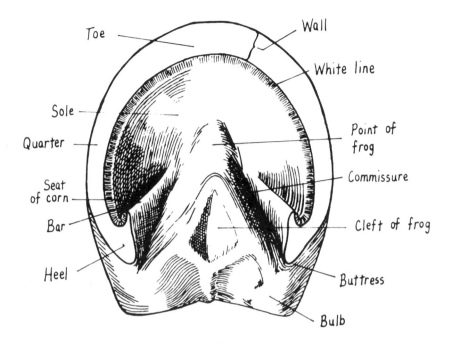

Toe

Wall

White line

Sole

Quarter

Point of frog

Seat of corn

Commissure

Bar

Cleft of frog

Heel

Buttress

Bulb

Ground surface of a normal front foot.

You can stand a horse in water or even wrap wet burlap sacks around his feet. If the horse is shod, a leather sole with packing beneath it may be used. An oil-based hoof dressing should be applied to help retain the natural moisture in the horse's hoof.

Q. Can I trim and shoe my own horse?

A. I don't advise it for the novice horseperson, especially if the horse has any kind of foot problem. If you're not experienced in doing this sort of thing, it is too easy to do the horse harm. What I would recommend for the horse-owner, particularly one who might have trouble getting the regular services of a farrier, is the use of a rasp. With a little help from your farrier you can learn to keep the foot wearing level between regular trimmings.

Q. Do different kinds of horses require different kinds of shoes?

A. Yes. The use the horse is put to will dictate what kind of shoes he will wear. A show horse would be shod differently from a race horse or a cutting horse because the type of work he does is entirely different.

Q. Does it hurt the horse to be trimmed?

A. It does not hurt to trim off excess hoof; it's like trimming off excess fingernail. Of course, if you trim too deep, that's another matter.

Q. What about shoeing? Is driving the nails painful?

A. If the nail is driven properly, there is no pain involved. Some horses object to the shock of the hammer, but once they become familiar with it, it would be the same as if someone were tapping on the bottom of your shoe with a hammer.

Q. Are dark hoofs stronger than light hoofs?

A. The color in a horse's hoof is dictated by pigment. In all my years of shoeing I cannot say that a foot of one color is stronger than the other just because of its color. The horse inherits the good structure, or poor structure, in his feet. Of course, the conditions in which he is forced to live and the work he must do has its effects. But I've seem as many good white feet as dark feet. If a horse doesn't have a good foot, it has nothing to do with color.

Q. Is it unusual for horses to have feet that are different from each other?

A. No. This is an inherited characteristic that is quite common. Frequently you will see a horse with a "dish" (concave) in one front foot and not in the other or one heel that is higher than the other. In such cases it might be necessary to trim him a little more often. But unless the difference is so marked that one foot could be considered deformed, it usually doesn't make much difference if the feet are trimmed so that they are at the same angles.

Q. Is it true that horses shed the frogs of their feet?

A. Yes. It's a natural thing. The part that isn't needed will be shed and grow back in a relatively short time. The excess sole also will flake off. If it doesn't, the farrier usually will trim it so that the sole doesn't strike the ground before the wall of the foot.

Q. Can a horse that "toes in" or "toes out" be trimmed or shod to help his way of going?

A. A horse that toes out should be trimmed more, or lowered, on the outside wall in order to turn the foot in. For the horse that toes in, more hoof should be taken off on the inside wall of the foot. However, you must take into consideration the horse's conformation and "way of going" and use care in not overcorrecting or it will cause excessive strain on the bone structure and joints.

A horse that has these types of faults should be trimmed more frequently or the condition will get worse. You must keep in mind that it is more important to trim the horse by the way he wears his feet than it is by the way he actually stands.

Q. I am going to do quite a bit of trail riding. Should my horse be shod?

A. Probably yes. I think a good rule would be, "Don't force your horse to walk barefooted anywhere you would not like to walk barefooted." Stony terrain or rough gravel is hard on your feet; it's also hard on your horse's feet. It's a good idea to carry a hoof pick when you're trail riding and to stop periodically to pick out his feet.

Q. What should I do if my horse pulls a shoe?

A. If the shoe is not completely off, take it off. It's dangerous to move a horse with the shoe half on. A loose nail could penetrate the sole, or he could otherwise damage himself. Walk the horse home, and call the farrier.

Q. Should a horse be shod for riding on ice and snow?

A. Only if he is ridden often. Then the shoes should have "ice points" made of barium to prevent slipping and pads to keep snow from balling up inside his foot. If you ride a horse barefooted, use silicone spray, oil, or grease on the underside of his foot to prevent balling.

Q. As an owner, what is my responsibility to the farrier when he comes to my barn?

A. If at all possible, it's best to have a shoeing area inside a building where the farrier can work out of the elements. There must be good lighting from the rear, because that's the direction the shoeing surface of the foot is facing when it is raised. The shoeing area should be located so that the farrier can pull his truck nearby. Having to run 300 feet everytime he needs something out of his truck can get to be a problem. Provide a flat surface for the horse to stand on.

If the horse is standing in half an inch of loose dirt or 3 inches of grass, the farrier can't get an accurate picture of how the horse is standing. If you don't have a cemented area, a heavy gauge piece of plywood capable of bearing the horse's weight works pretty well.

The owner or attendant should be present when the farrier is there to tell the shoer if the horse has any problems, such as forging or interfering. If the farrier doesn't know the problem, he can't correct it. Another good reason for having a handler present is to keep the horse under control. Many times just the presence of the owner keeps the horse reassured and quiet.

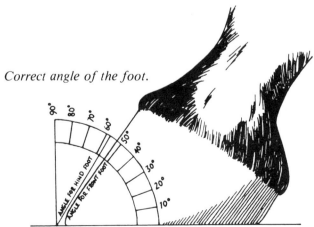

Correct angle of the foot.

It also is helpful if the owner has conditioned the horse by handling his feet in the same manner that the shoer does before the horse is trimmed. That way it is easier for the horse to accept the farrier. This is especially important for the young horse. If the owner works with him a little bit every day, by the time the farrier gets there to do his job the horse is familiar and relaxed with his foot in a restrained position.

It's also a good idea to tap the bottom of the foot lightly with a hammer. This will prepare him for the first time he gets shoes put on.

If the horse is shod in the cross-ties, they should be loose enough to allow some freedom of movement. Most horses will not stand on three legs if their heads are held in too rigid a position. If the horse is not cross-tied, he can be held by an attendant. There should be enough room in the shoeing area so that if the horse does create a disturbance, there is ample space for the farrier to move away.

If insects are a problem, the horse should be covered with a sheet and insect repellent should be applied. If the horse is not being attacked by flies or mosquitoes he is going to be a lot more comfortable. This makes it easier for the handler and the farrier is certainly going to be happier.

Q. How can I find a good farrier?

A. Probably the best way is to visit a reputable stable or knowledgeable horseperson and ask. Or perhaps your veterinarian could refer you to someone who is competent. If not properly done, shoeing can produce many problems for the foot. It is possible to ruin a good horse in a very short period of time by bad shoeing. It is also possible to cure or relieve some forms of lameness by proper shoeing.

10
"Vetting" the Horse

Dennis B. Pinkston of Swartz Creek, Michigan, cares for animals. He is engaged in the private practice of veterinary medicine as well as being county veterinarian for Genesee County, Michigan. He is owner, breeder, trainer, and driver of Standardbred racing horses and is a "mender" of various and sundry creatures who have been thrown away or found injured by the side of the road.

Many of these animals have taken permanent residence with the Pinkston family, who currently host six dogs, seven cats, a goat, a raccoon, a twenty-year-old stray pony, and a quail. Anyone who knows Pinkston can vouch for the fact that he is, indeed, an "animal person," by vocation as well as avocation.

According to Pinkston, at least 95 percent of the people who own horses shouldn't.

"They don't know how to take care of them," he says, "and they don't care enough about them to learn. Time and time again I see the poor beasts turned out in a patch of weeds that the owners calls a pasture. Half the time they don't even have water to drink. And these stupid owners think they are taking care of their horses.

"Goodness knows for what reason most people buy a horse in the first place. Maybe they think it will gratify their own faltering ego in some way. Once the newness wears off, the pathetic animal is left to take care of himself the best way he can."

"Unfortunately, there's no way a horse cooped up in a stall or a crummy little pasture can do it. The horse has been taken away from his natural way of life, and he can't survive unless his owner takes care of him. He is totally dependent".

"I see the same thing happening every day with small animals . . . dogs and cats mostly. Parents rush out and find a female cat so their children can see how things are born. Later they load up the cat and kittens and drop them off by the side of the road to starve to death. I really don't know what these parents think they are teaching the kids, except a total disregard for living things in general, and animals in particular".

"Then, again, this same kind of person will go out and get a dog that is supposed to teach the kid responsibility. I don't know why they think the dog can succeed where they have failed, and most of the time it's a bust. The kid doesn't want to learn responsibility in the first place. He'd rather be out playing ball or loafing around."

"Feeding and cleaning up after a dog, to say nothing of training him, gets to be a big drag, so that poor beast, too, winds up chained to some sort of dog house, living in his own filth, shivering at 20 degrees below zero. Sometimes he is fed, sometimes not. Often he is turned loose to run the neighborhood, dumped by the side of the road, or brought to the animal control center for us to take care of or kill."

"No. Most people shouldn't have animals. They aren't concerned enough to take care of them. They're too much responsibility for the average person. It takes a special kind of person to be an 'animal' person, even more special to be a 'horse' person. The horse is a large animal that requires a particular kind of care. It takes a unique, exceptional kind of person to do it and do it well. Only that kind of person can be called a real horse person."

The following questions were posed to Pinkston by novice horsepersons:

Q. What's the best way to take care of a horse?
A. That's a broad question, but it has a simple answer. The best way to take care of a horse, or any other animal for that matter, is to use common sense and treat the horse the way you would like to be treated.
Q. *What is the normal temperature for a horse?*
A. 99.5 to 100.5 degrees. Over 101 degrees indicates illness.
Q. How do you take a horse's temperature?
A. Rectally, the same as you would a dog or a cat, or a baby for that matter. Use a blunt-ended thermometer; put a little petroleum jelly on it, and insert it in the horse's rectum. Keep a firm hold on it; two

minutes will give you a temperature reading. You can use a regular people-type thermometer, or get a larger one specifically made for large animals. These are easier to use because you can keep a better hold on them. Many have an "eye" or a "ring" at the end to which you can attach a loop of string.

Q. What equipment do I need that might help the veterinarian?

A. Most vets come prepared with the tools and materials that they will need. The owner can help the most by having the horse in the barn or box stall, out of the rain or snow. In a stall the vet can get hold of the horse. It's also necessary to have good light, warm water, and a good halter on the horse.

Q. Am I expected to help the veterinarian?

A. Normally not. Most veterinarians don't expect the owner to be equipped mentally or physically to be of much assistance. Generally the vet assumes that he is going to do most of the work himself. If he thinks he is going to have a problem, he will have an assistant with him.

The owner should be there when the vet arrives so he doesn't have to go chasing out in the pasture to get the horse and so the vet can discuss the animal's symptoms and condition. The owner then will have the advantage of asking the veterinarian any questions he might have relative to the continued treatment he might have to perform and will have a better idea of the horse's condition and ailment. It is much easier, and certainly more satisfactory, to explain something person to person than to write it in a note.

Q. Do horses have problems with their teeth?

A. Yes. Frequently they have problems when they are two or three years old and then again when they are four or five years old. Their baby teeth are falling out, and their permanent teeth are coming in. Sometimes these new teeth wear unevenly or are sharp and ragged. If they are, and if they're bothering the horse, they will have to be filed or floated. As a horse gets up around ten or eleven years old, his teeth may not be wearing evenly and may become sharp and ragged, causing him irritation. The age would vary, depending on the kind of food the horse eats and the kind of care he has had. I'd say it is very important for every horse who has a little age on him to have his teeth checked regularly.

Q. What are wolf teeth?

A. Wolf teeth are vestigial teeth that all horses don't have. Actually, they are called the first pre-molar and are positioned in front of the first large pre-molar. Generally, if they come through, they give the horse problems. This is especially true with a harness horse because of the position of the overcheck bit. It would be a fair assumption that if you are having "bitting" problems with your horse, if he is tossing his head or going "sour" on his bits, he is having problems with his teeth.

Q. Is it true that a horse with a broken leg must be destroyed?

A. The term "broken leg" is a very broad one. There are all kinds of broken legs, and some of them might not be reparable. However, most fractures are of the lower leg and often can be pinned or plated successfully. With the advances in medicine and surgical techniques, we are able to repair many conditions that used to be considered hopeless.

The case of the great Thoroughbred racing mare Ruffian points out a problem. She died of postoperative shock, not the fact that her leg couldn't be set. If she hadn't been the hyper-type of individual that she was, the leg could have been repaired.

Q. Do you use tranquilizers in the practice of equine medicine?

A. I use them frequently, especially in treating the highly excitable animal. The tranquilizers we use today are really quite safe. They have improved tremendously over the early ones.

Q. How old should a colt be before he is castrated?

A. A colt can be castrated, or neutered, anytime, but normally after he is six months old. I don't recommend it in the middle of the summer or when insects are a problem, but that has nothing to do with how old the horse is.

We're always quick to castrate a bad-natured stallion, but very few people consider spaying a problem mare. Sometimes they have ovarian problems, cysts, tumors, and the like. Often what is called bad temperament in a mare can be traced back to this problem.

Q. What kind of a horse should be left a stallion?

A. Only the finest horses in the breed should be left whole and used at stud. Far too many horses of inferior quality are being left intact and used at stud. This does nothing but downgrade the breed. The same is true of mares. People seem to think that just because a mare is a female she should be bred. That just isn't true. Only the best horses of either sex should be used for breeding purposes.

Q. What shots should my horse have?

A. That would vary in large part on the area of the country in which you live and what, if any, problems you have in that area. Regardless of area, however, I would recommend tetanus, viral abortion (Rhinopneumonitis), and equine influenza. When you get into encephalomyelitis (eastern, western, Venezuelan), it pretty much depends on infection in an area. You would have to rely on your veterinarian for advice.

Q. Are young horses more susceptible to disease than older horses?

A. Yes. The same thing is true of animals of any species. Young animals have to be exposed before they are able to build up antibodies that will protect them at a later age.

Q. Does a horse that is heavily used need more veterinary care than a horse that is only used occasionally?

A. I doubt it. I really believe just the opposite. I think that a horse that is used, exercised, and taken care of properly probably needs less vet work than an animal that is used only occasionally.

Q. How can I find a good horse veterinarian?

A. That same question could be applied to finding a good doctor for your family. I think word of mouth is the best. You might start by asking other horse-owners in your area or your farrier. If there is a veterinarian who treats only small animals nearby, ask him. You are going to hear god things about the vet that is doing a good job. If he's not doing a good job, you're going to hear about that individual, too.

Q. What medical supplies should I keep on hand in my barn?

A. You should keep a good topical antiseptic such as iodine. I prefer one of the tamed iodines such as povidone. Tamed iodines have all the chemical properties of iodine, yet do not bite or blister the way tincture or iodine can. Hydrogen peroxide is a good flushing agent for a wound. A good antibiotic ointment, spray, powder, or liquid, such as Furacin, is excellent for use on a wound that might have to be sutured. Scarlet oil, gentian violet, iodine, or many of the other antiseptics have a cauterizing action. In some cases these can do more harm than good.

Iodine for an area that is impossible to suture, such as a puncture of the foot, is beyond a doubt the best thing you can use.

Q. Is it better for a foal to be born in a stall or in the pasture?

A. During the warm spring and summer months the most natural and ideal place for foaling is a clean, open pasture, away from other livestock. Under good pasture conditions there is less danger of either infection or mechanical injury to the mare and foal. It is important, however, that the ground be dry and warm. A colt born outdoors in a cold spring rainstorm invites trouble. Small paddocks that are muddy and dirty with fecal droppings are highly unsatisfactory.

Q. What is the average life span of the horse?

A. I believe the oldest verified age of a horse is somewhere around fifty years old, but that would be quite unusual. An average for a horse given good care would be somewhere around twenty-five years old.

Q. What are chestnuts?

A. Chestnuts are vestigial tissue that serve no known function. They are simply prehistoric leftovers of what was once an appendage, such as a thumb.

Q. Can the horse's age be determined by his teeth?

A. One who is experienced can come pretty close in most cases, even though the teeth will vary with the individual horse, the kind of feed he gets and the care he has had. With more purebred horses being bred, it's getting so that you don't have to rely on the teeth any more: you have the registration papers.

A. Temporary incisors to ten days of age: first or central upper and lower temporary incisors appear. Courtesy United States Department of Agriculture.

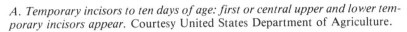

A.

B. Temporary incisors at four to six weeks of age. Second or intermediate upper and lower temporary incisors appear. Courtesy United States Department of Agriculture.

C. Temporary incisors at six to ten months. Third or corner upper and lower temporary incisors appear. Courtesy United States Department of Agriculture.

B.

D. Temporary incisors at one year. Crowns of central temporary incisors show wear. Courtesy United States Department of Agriculture.

E. Temporary incisors at one to one and one-half years. Intermediate temporary incisors show wear. Courtesy United States Department of Agriculture.

F. Temporary incisors at two years. All show wear. Courtesy United States Department of Agriculture.

C.

G. Incisors at four years. Permanent incisors replace temporary centrals and intermediates; temporary corner incisors remain. Courtesy United States Department of Agriculture.

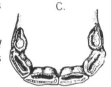

H. Incisors at five years. All permanent; cups in all incisors. Courtesy United States States Department of Agriculture.

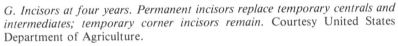

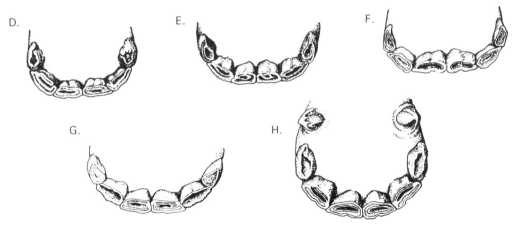

D.   E.   F.

G.   H.

I. Incisors at six years. Cups worn out of lower central incisors. Courtesy United States Department of Agriculture.

J. Incisors at seven years. Cups worn out of lower intermediate incisors. Courtesy United States Department of Agriculture.

K. Incisors at eight years. Cups worn out of all lower incisors, and dental star (dark line in front of cup) appears on lower central and intermediate pairs. Courtesy United States Department of Agriculture.

L. Incisors at nine years. Cups worn out of upper central incisors; dental star on upper central and intermediate pairs. Courtesy United States Department of Agriculture.

M. Incisors at ten years. Cups worn out of upper intermediate incisors, and dental star is present in all incisors. Courtesy United States Department of Agriculture.

N. Incisors at eleven or twelve years. Cups worn in all incisors (smooth mouthed), and dental star approaches center of cups. Courtesy United States Department of Agriculture.

O. Characteristic shape of lower incisors at eighteen years. Courtesy United States Department of Agriculture.

P.

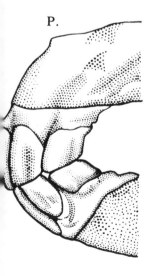
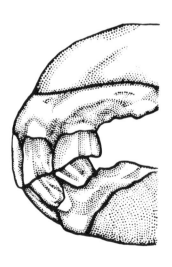

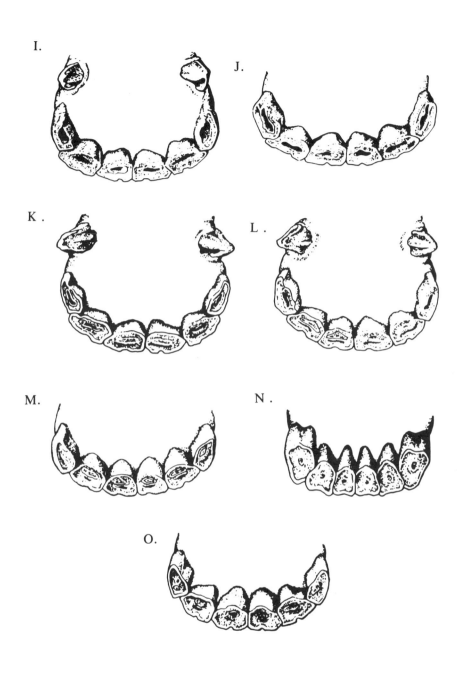

P. Side view of five, seven, and twenty-year-old mouth. Note that as the horse advances in age, the teeth change from nearly perpendicular to slanting sharply toward the front. Courtesy United States Department of Agriculture.

11
Internal Parasites

By definition a parasite is a plant or animal living on, in, or with another living organism (the host), from whom the parasite obtains food and shelter. External types include flies, ticks, mites, mange, ringworm, and lice. The internal types, which will be discussed here, include ascarids, stomach worms, pinworms, bots, and strongyles or blood worms. More than 150 different kinds of parasites have been found to infest horses, including 57 species of internal parasites. Is it any wonder that the horse's fight for survival is perpetual and can be costly to him?

The symptoms of the presence of worm parasites in your horse are usually not spectacular. However, the horse will show decreased work efficiency, poor utilization of food, and his coat will be rough and dull. Parasites are one of the causes of colic; they also may be the cause of intermittent lameness and may produce a chronic cough and bronchitis. Occasionally death will even occur due to a blood clot.

Some adult worms produce toxins that destroy red blood cells, leading to an anemic condition, and immature worms migrating through the body tissues open the way for bacteria and fungi to enter, causing other serious problems and diseases.

Medical treatment, or worming, for internal parasites is necessary, but it is only a small part of the total parasite control program. Major emphasis must be placed on *prevention*. Internal parasites gain entry into the horse's body in the form of eggs, larvae, or adults. The parasites already present in the horse's body will have to be killed by drugs, but the purpose of a good control program is to break the life cycle of the parasite. The following practices are effective in reducing parasite numbers:

1. Clean stall and rebed as often as possible, thus reducing the chance of internal parasites getting on feeds from fecal materials.

2. Remove manure from premises daily, and either spread it on a field where horses will not graze for a year or where the field will be plowed and reseeded before horses have contact with it.

3. If manure must be left near the barn, keep it in a covered pit where it can heat, thereby killing parasite eggs and larvae. This will also prevent a major source of fly breeding.

4. If the floor of the stall is earth, remove the top layer at least once a year and replace it with clean soil.

5. Do not feed grain or hay from the floor of the stall. Use a feed box and manger or hay rack. This will help prevent contamination of feeds with manure, which may contain large numbers of parasite eggs and/or larvae.

6. Keep good clean water available for your horse, and do not allow him to drink from barnyard pools or water holes in the pasture. Manure drainage into these areas make them an excellent source of internal parasite contamination.

7. Avoid overstocking and overgrazing of pastures. Rotate as much as possible, because more parasites are present at the bottom inch of grass. It is better to have two smaller pastures than one large one, because the rotating pastures helps break the life cycle of the parasite.

8. Small exercise yards should not contain pasture grasses that encourage the horse to eat contaminated material. It is best to have them graveled and to pick up droppings frequently.

9. In the pasture it is advisable to practice frequent mowing and chain harrowing.

10. Grain should be kept in covered containers away from flies, birds, and rodents which may carry parasites from farm to farm.

Drugs used to eliminate internal parasites from the horse's body are of necessity potent medications. They should be used carefully and under the direction of a competent veterinarian.

The general rule for worming adult horses is to do it in the fall after the first killing frost and again in the spring. If your horse has a high-level internal parasite problem, your veterinarian may recommend more frequent worming. The recommended worming for foals is in four doses: June, August, October, and December.

BOT FLIES

It is the habit of the bot fly to hover about the horse and then quickly dart toward the animal, usually the front legs, where the females will glue individual eggs to the hair in a matter of seconds. The female usually lays up to 500 eggs.

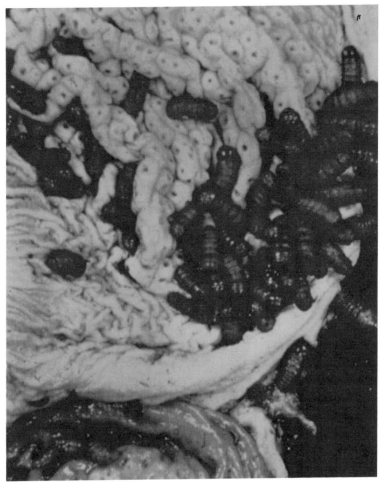

Bot Larva. Courtesy Michigan State University, Large Animal Clinic.

The horse tends to lick himself where the eggs are attached, stimulating hatching. The newly hatched larvae are then taken into the horse's mouth in this manner. Some larvae burrow into the tongue and migrate through the body until they finally arrive in the stomach, where they attach themselves to the stomach wall. In ten to eleven months they mature in the stomach, release their hold on the stomach wall, and pass out with the feces. The mature larvae burrow into the ground and change into pupa stage. In fifteen to seventeen days the mature bot fly emerges, mates, and begins the cycle again.

STOMACH WORMS

There are at least ten different types of stomach worms, several of which are known to cause lesions, creating inflamation of the walls of the stomach. In the horse's stomach adult worms lay eggs which are passed out with the feces. In larvae form they reinfest the horse through the mouth, are swallowed, and mature into adult worms in the horse's stomach to repeat the cycle.

ASCARIDS (Intestinal Worms)

In the small intestine adult worms lay eggs which pass out with the feces. The eggs are swallowed by grazing horses. The embryos are liberated in the small intestine, penetrate the gut wall, and migrate to the heart and lungs and then to the throat. There they are once again swallowed, and the worms develop to maturity in the small intestine. Adult worms reach 9 to 12 inches in length.

STRONGYLES (Blood Worms, Palasade Worms)

There are many species of strongyles infecting horses. Most of them are less than an inch long and hardly visible to the naked eye. They attach themselves within the host, sucking blood. The female worms deposit large number of eggs which leave the horse with the feces.

In their larvae stage they are swallowed by grazing horses and, depending upon their species, migrate to various organs in the horse's body. Those that attach themselves to the walls of the arteries are responsible for certain types of lameness and even death due to blocking blood flow in the arteries or embolism.

PINWORMS

Pinworms are frequently seen in the manure of infected animals.

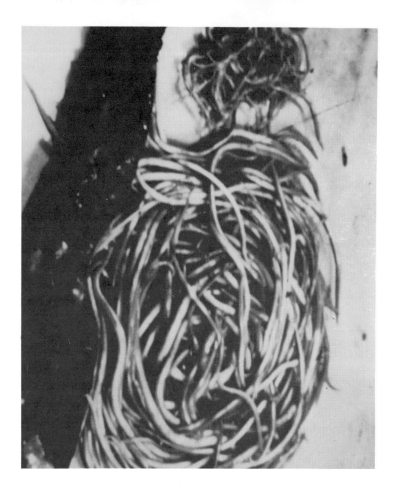

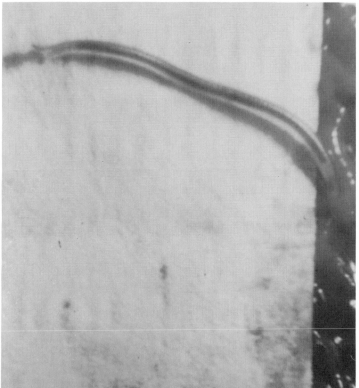

Ascarids protruding from ruptured small intestine. Courtesy Michigan State University, Large Animal Clinic.

They are white and approximately 2 to 3 inches long. The worms mature in the large intestines and work their way outward through the rectum. The irritation causes infested animals to rub against fences or other solid objects. Usually the eggs develop in manure and reinfest the animal as he grazes to repeat the cycle.

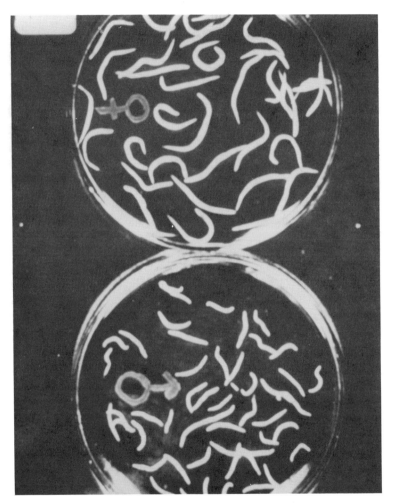

Strongyloides. Male and female. Courtesy Michigan State University, Large Animal Clinic.

Adult bloodworm attached to the mucosa of the colon. Courtesy Michigan State University, Large Animal Clinic.

12
Diseases of the Horse

Preventing disease is more effective than treating your horse after he is sick. In the first place, you have a responsibility to all animals entrusted in your care to protect them from injury, sickness, and pain. Second, any time your horse is ill it will prevent you from using him. Third, if your horse needs treatment, it will usually cost you time and money.

The horse industry, taken as a whole, expends tens of thousands of dollars each year because horse-owners do not follow the prescribed practices of good breeding, feeding, management, and disease prevention.

Most preventative measures are simply good common-sense ideas with scientific principles behind them. Animal scientists have discovered many practices that horse-owners find beneficial in the maintenance of healthy horses. There are many fine drugs, vaccines, disinfectants, and other products manufactured today that can be used successfully to help keep your horse healthy. Fortunately, most people in the field of veterinary medicine are ready and willing to help in the wise use of these materials so that you can set up a sound health program for your horse.

As a general health program, check the following:

1. Avoid public feeding and watering facilities.

2. Establish a scheduled vaccination program as a disease-prevention measure.

3. If signs of infectious disease appear, isolate affected animals promptly, provide them with separate water and feed containers, and follow the instructions and prescribed treatment of your veterinarian.

4. Provide good sanitation and a high level of nutrition.

5. Follow a scheduled internal and external parasite control program.

The following comments on ailments and diseases common to the horse are intended only as a guide for the horse-owner. Their purpose is to make you aware of early symptoms so you can spot trouble as quickly as possible.

At the first sign of illness in your horse you should call a veterinarian for diagnosis and treatment. In most cases, the more prompt the treatment, the more successful it will be. It can mean the difference between saving your horse and being forced to have him destroyed.

Tetanus (commonly called lockjaw). Tetanus is caused by contaminated wounds. Puncture wounds are the most serious, but any wound (such as a saddle gall or laceration) that is contaminated with foreign matter may result in a fatal tetanus infection. The disease is characterized by stiffness in one or more muscles. In advanced stages the reflexes are increased and the animal is easily frightened into violent spasms by sudden movement or noise. Sweating and high fever occur. Death is usually caused by asphyxiation produced by spasms of the muscles that control respiration.

Once a horse is infected with tetanus it is usually fatal. Therefore a systematic program of immunization with tetanus toxoid is of utmost importance. Two initial doses of tetanus toxoid to the foal at four- to eight -week intervals should be given. Then immunity should be maintained by booster doses each year to provide excellent protection against tetanus.

Equine Encephalomyelitis (commonly called sleeping sickness, blind staggers, or brain fever). This is an acute viral disease affecting birds and many mammals, including humans and is characterized by central nervous disturbances and a high death rate. Signs of this disease include high fever, partial loss of vision, lack of coordination, yawning, grinding of teeth, drowsiness, sagging lower lip, and the inability to swallow.

In late stages the horse is unable to rise, becomes paralyzed, and dies. Death usually results in about 50 percent of the cases, and those that do not die may be permanently afflicted by nerve damage.

There are three separate strains of virus causing the disease in the United States: Eastern, Western, and Venezuelan. Immunity from one type does not result in immunity to either of the others, and none of these types is geographically restricted. The disease is transmitted by mosquitoes. Therefore, insect control is highly important. Since there is no effective treatment of the disease once the animal is infected, all equines should be vaccinated for each type. Consult your veterinarian.

Strangles (also called distemper). This is a contagious disease caused by a bacterial organism. It is most commonly transmitted through contact with other horses and from feed and water troughs. Generally this is an upper respiratory infection involving the nose, sinuses, pharynx, and glands of the head and neck area. Symptoms include high temperature, increased respiratory rate, nasal discharge, lack of appetite, and restlessness.

These symptoms are usually followed by swelling of the lymph nodes of the head and throat. They later abcess, rupture, and discharge an infectious, puslike material. Infection may spread throughout the body, resulting in chronic infection or death. Ordinarily, with good nursing care the infection remains localized in the tissues of the head and upper neck.

Affected animals should be isolated, and strict sanitary measures should be employed. Complete rest is essential, and the affected animal should be protected from cold, inclement weather, and drafts. Younger animals are most susceptible to this disease. However, older animals that have not previously been exposed or those whose resistance has decreased may be infected. Consult your veterinarian for treatment. Vaccination for Strangles is now available which will greatly reduce the incidence of this disease and will provide immunity for one year.

Equine Influenza. This is a highly contagious virus disease occurring in horses of all ages, but particularly younger horses. Equine influenza appears suddenly with the horse showing an elevated temperature, loss of appetite, and depression. Muscular weakness and tremors are not uncommon, and there may be swelling of the lower surface and extremities along with inflamation of the tendon sheaths. A watery nasal discharge may later change to a thick yellowish mucus, and the lymph glands of the head and neck may become swollen.

Fatalities are rare, provided the infected horse is kept at complete rest and the disease does not become complicated by bacterial infection. Antibiotics or sulfa drugs are not effective in controlling the virus, but they do help prevent secondary infection. The virus itself seems to run its course regardless of the treatment. Vaccine is available for use in controlling this disease. Two shots six to twelve weeks apart followed by one booster shot each year provides immunization.

Hernia (rupture). A hernia is the protrusion of an internal organ through the wall of the containing cavity. The term commonly means the passage of intestine or omentum through an opening in the abdominal muscles. This type of hernia is usually caused by overexertion or a severe blow or kick. Death will occur if the hernial opening swells around the loop of intestine so that the circulation and passage of the intestinal contents are stopped.

Umbilical, scrotal, and inguinal hernias are fairly common in young foals, but they sometimes disappear with age. In stallions, scrotal and inguinal hernias are often fatal if they become strangulated. Mares affected with any type of hernia should not be used for breeding. Surgery cures many hernias. However, the operation is usually a major one in which there is always an element of danger.

Anthrax. Anthrax is an acute infectious disease more common in cows than in horses. Infected animals are feverish, excitable, and later depressed. They carry the head low and breathe rapidly. Swelling appears over the body and around the neck. There may be a bloody discharge from the body openings.

Isolate sick animals at the first sign of any of the above symptoms, and call a veterinarian at once. Large quantities of antibiotics may be helpful, and in the early stages of the disease, an anti-anthrax serum may help. All healthy animals should be vaccinated. In infected areas vaccination should be repeated every year and fly control should be provided.

Equine Infectious Anemia (swamp fever). This is an infectious virus disease. Symptoms may vary but usually include some of the following: high and intermittent fever, depression, stiffness and weakness especially in the hind quarters, anemia, jaundice, edema and swelling of the lower body and legs, and loss of weight and condition even though the appetite is good. Most affected animals die within two to four weeks.

No successful treatment is known for this disease, and at the present time there is no preventive vaccination. To control this disease sick animals must be destroyed and their carcasses burned or buried. The only prevention possible is to practice good sanitation and eliminate or reduce biting insects as much as possible.

Navel Infection (joint ill, navel ill). This is an infectious disease of newborn animals caused by several kinds of bacteria. Infected animals have a loss of appetite, swelling, soreness and stiffness of the joints, general listlessness, and umbilical swelling and discharge. About 50 percent of infected foals die, and many or those who survive have deformed joints. Providing clean quarters for the newborn and painting the navel cord and feet with iodine are the best preventive measures.

Azoturia (Monday morning sickness). This malady is seen most often when horses are kept in stalls, fed highly, and worked regularly with infrequent one or two day rests. The highly fed horse, when ridden after a day or two of no use, may have some difficulty in collecting himself or shifting his balance.

The symptoms appear suddenly, usually when he has traveled only a short distance. This stiffness will very rapidly increase, accompanied by sweating and blowing. If the horse is forced to continue he will soon be unable to use his hindquarters.

At the first sign of azoturia stop the horse and dismount. *Do not move the horse!* Blanket the animal at once, and keep him quiet. Call the veterinarian for treatment. This disease is rarely serious if the horse is stopped and kept comfortable at the first sign of trouble. However, even the most skillful veterinarian cannot save an animal that has been forced to move after the onset of difficulty.

Colic. Colic is a general term describing a set of symptoms that indicate severe or violent abdominal pain. Colic can be the result of innumerable causes, but it is frequently connected with irregular feeding or the feeding of improper food, long fasts followed by the allowance of extra large feeds, a sudden change of diet, large amounts of cold water consumed by a hot horse, improper cooling of a hot horse, or obstruction of the bowel.

The horse with colic is apt to bite at his sides or kick at his abdomen, roll frequently, and get up and down in his stall. Sweating often occurs with the pulse hard and accelerated if acute spasms are present. Breathing may become hurried.

Colic is far more common in horses than in any other animal. The reason for this frequency has been attributed to the small size of the stomach, the inability to vomit, the large size of the intestines and the puckering which allows food or foreign bodies to lodge within the abdomen, and the frequency with which the horse is affected with internal parasites. Last, but certainly not least, is the fact that the horse has to work at the direction of his owner.

Place the horse showing symptoms of colic in a roomy box stall which is well bedded. Allow the animal his freedom, but ensure that there is nothing present that is liable to cause injury. Call the veterinarian immediately.

Rhinopneumonitis (equine abortion, viral abortion, contagious abortion). Rhinopneumonitis is an equine respiratory disease caused by a virus similar to that responsible for the common cold in humans. It is acute and highly contagious and characterized by respiratory infection in young horses and abortion in pregnant mares. Abortion can be prevented by inoculation each year.

13
Common Unsoundnesses of the Horse

DEFECTIVE EYES

The eyes can be examined best with a flashlight in a darkened stall or by standing the horse in daylight in an open doorway. Cataracts or cloudiness of the cornea are usually easily detected, while other defects may not be so easily observed. However, the general expression of the head, unnatural carriage of the ears, or frequent stumbling or shying may indicate poor eyesight. A watery eye should always be suspect.

WATCH EYE (GLASS EYE, WALL EYE)

These terms are applied to a horse's eye whose iris is white because it lacks pigment. This eye is just as functional as the normal-colored eye and should not be confused with blindness.

PARROT MOUTH

Faulty conformation where the upper incisor teeth overlap the lower. If the condition is mild, it will cause no serious problem. However, if the condition is severe, it can interfere with the horse's ability to graze and chew his food. For treatment, keep the lower incisors shortened by rasping and the molars trimmed level.

UNDERSHOT JAW

Faulty conformation where the lower incisor teeth overlap the upper. This condition can cause the same problems as parrot mouth. To help alleviate this condition the upper incisors should be shortened by rasping and the molars trimmed level.

POLL-EVIL

Inflamed swelling of the poll between the ears. It usually follows a severe bruise of the poll or is the result of a tightly fitting halter or bridle. This should always be regarded as serious. Many cases of poll-evil can be cured. However, treatment usually must be continued for many weeks under the direction of a veterinarian.

FISTULA OF THE WITHERS

Inflamed swelling of the withers usually resulting from a severe bruise or irritation. It first appears as a large, hot, painful swelling upon the withers, which finally ruptures, allowing pus to escape. Some fistulas heal, leaving a large fibrous tumor, but most continue to discharge pus and show no tendency to heal. Many of these cases can be successfully treated and cured by a veterinarian. However, treatment often must be continued for many weeks.

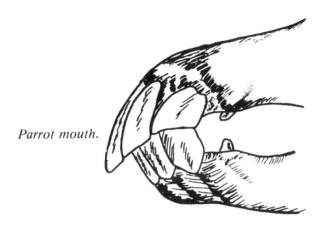

Parrot mouth.

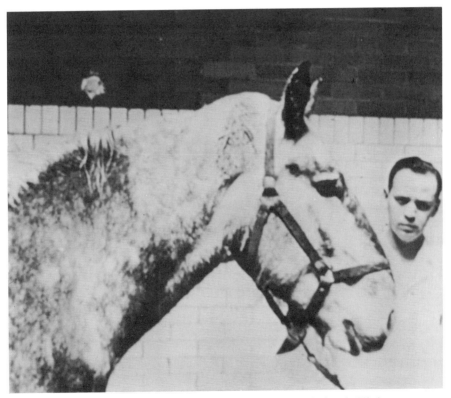

Poll-evil. Courtesy Michigan State University, Large Animal Clinic.

Sweeney of the shoulder. Courtesy Michigan State University, Large Animal Clinic.

SWEENEY

Sweeney is the atrophy (decrease in size) of a muscle or group of muscles, usually of the shoulder but also of the hip. This condition often is caused by a blow, severe strain, ill-fitting collar, or lameness. Sweeney of the hip may follow an attack of azoturia or difficulty in foaling. Some cases of sweeney recover after an extended period of rest. Blisters and irritants applied under the close supervision of a veterinarian may hasten recovery.

SHOE BOIL (CAPPED ELBOW)

This is a swelling at the point of the elbow. It is usually caused by constant irritation of the heel (or shoe) upon the point of the elbow when the horse lies down with the front leg flexed beneath the body. Recovery usually follows proper treatment.

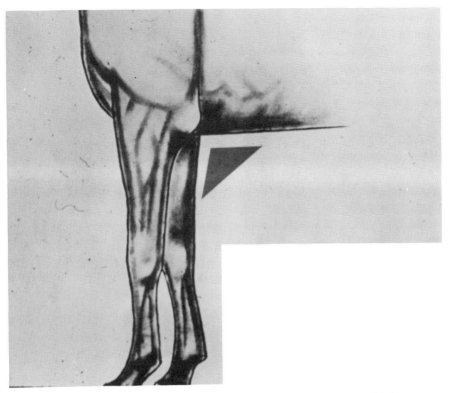

Shoe boil. Courtesy Michigan State University, Large Animal Clinic.

SPLINT

This is a hard, bony enlargement usually found on the inside of the front cannon bone of young horses. The splint can occur on the outside of the front cannon bone but is rarely seen on the rear legs. It often results from a kick, overexertion, or concussion produced by working on hard surfaces. Splints may occur on rapidly growing young horses but will frequently disappear as the animal grows older.

Splints.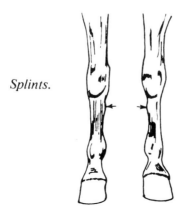

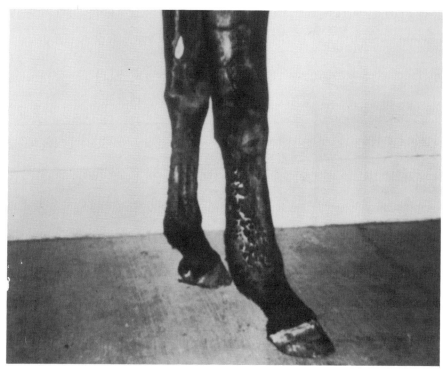

Bowed tendon. Courtesy Michigan State University, Large Animal Clinic.

BOWED TENDON

A bowed tendon is a sprain of the tendon on the back of the cannon bone above the fetlock. The swelling is soft in the early stages and hard in the late ones. This condition is usually caused by fatigue, overexertion, unequal weight distribution on a foot and leg, racing around turns, lack of conditioning, or poor track surface. The treatment involves complete rest. Consult your veterinarian for specific treatment. Surgical procedures are available to help relieve severe conditions. Pathological shoeing may be of help.

WIND-PUFF (WIND-GALL, ROAD-GALL, ROAD-PUFF)

Wind-galls are soft puffy swellings which usually occur on each side of the tendons above the fetlock or knee. They are common in young horses and in light breeds. They may be caused by strain, overexertion, or infectious disease. Wind-galls are not usually considered serious since they most often disappear and cause no lameness.

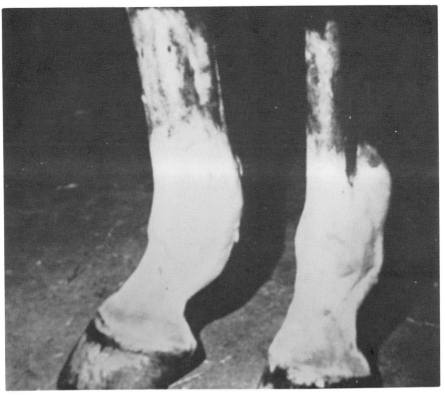

Left-low bowed tendon. Right-wind-puff. Courtesy Michigan State University, Large Animal Clinic.

RINGBONE

Ringbone is a hard, bony growth on either or both of the bones of the pastern, varying in size. The outlines of the right and left pasterns should be compared, or ringbone can be felt by carefully running the hand over the pastern. Lameness usually develops gradually but may appear quickly after a severe strain. The lameness is not necessarily in proportion to the size of the growth. It is the location of the swelling that is of most importance. Ringbone at the front or rear of the pastern usually produces severe lameness, because it interferes with the free movement of the tendons. At the side of the pastern it is usually less serious. Lameness always results if the joints become involved and there is no treatment which will remove the bony enlargement. Firing or blistering may cause the bones of the diseased joints to grow together, relieving the pain, or nerving is occasionally performed as a last resort.

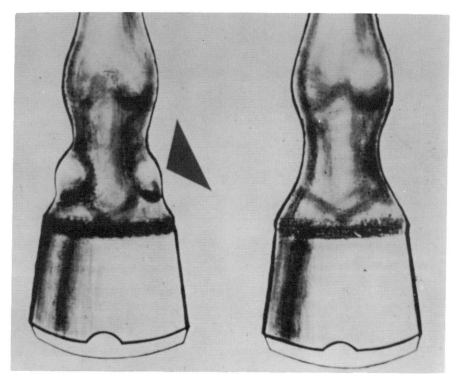

Ringbone. Courtesy Michigan State University, Large Animal Clinic.

SIDEBONE

Sidebones usually occur on the front feet as a result of injury or heavy work on hard surfaces and are an ossification of the lateral cartilage of the foot. Sidebones vary greatly in size and severity, and if lameness occurs it is usually not severe.

NAVICULAR DISEASE

This is an incurable condition involving the inflamation of the small navicular bone and bursa inside the hoof behind the coffin bone and the small pastern bone of the front foot. The symptoms are "pointing" of the toe when at rest and a short, stubby stride which gives the impression that the horse is lame in the shoulder.

LAMINITIS (FOUNDER)

An inflamation of the feet arising from any number of causes which

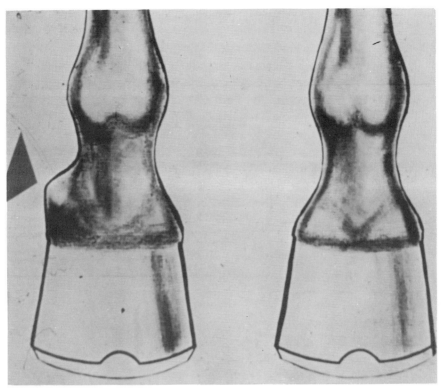

Sidebone. Courtesy Michigan State University, Large Animal Clinic.

Cross section of the foot illustrating the changes in bone structure as a result of laminitis. Note: the foundered foot has been correctively trimmed.

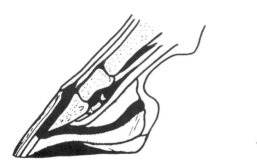

NORMAL FOOT   FOUNDERED FOOT

effect structural changes that most often result in permanent lameness and deformity. Laminitis can be caused from excessive grain or lush pasture, overwork, large amounts of cold water while the animal is hot, or improper cooling of a hot animal.

Acute cases show inflamation of the sensitive laminae on one or more feet, sensitivity to touch, lameness, pain on standing, a temperature to 106 degrees, sweating, and general distress caused by the pain of internal pressure of the foot. In acute cases apply a cold pack to feet or stand the horse in a cold mud bath and call the veterinarian. Horses that are kept stabled for long periods without proper exercise and kept on a high maintenance diet may be affected with laminitis.

QUARTER CRACK (SAND CRACK)

This is a vertical split in the wall of the hoof which can result from a dry brittle hoof or improper shoeing. Proper treatment and shoeing by any expert farrier (often in conjunction with the veterinarian if abcessing is involved) will hasten recovery. Lameness sometimes remains until the new growth of hoof is complete.

QUITTOR

Often the first sign of a quittor is a painful lameness. In looking for a cause, you may find a very tender area on the coronary band. If the condition develops into the formation of a quittor, lameness will increase and there will be considerable pain, heat, and swelling.

When the lesion matures and bursts there will be a measure of relief along with the draining of pus. However, the abcess will not heal as long as the decayed tissue remains intact. The severity of this unsoundness depends on the structure of the tissues involved. All cases must be considered serious, and a veterinarian should be consulted for treatment. Many cases require a surgical procedure.

CRACKED HEEL (GREASE HEEL, SCRATCHES)

These conditions are an inflammation of the posterior surfaces of the fetlocks, characterized by extensive scab formations. They are seen particularly in wet, cold weather and are frequently associated with poor (dirty) horse management. In its early stages clipping away the fetlock hair, washing the affected area with a medicated soap, drying it, and applying zinc ointment will suffice. In advanced stages, consult your veterinarian.

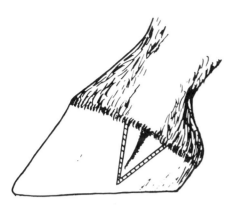

Quarter crack.

Quittor. Courtesy Michigan State University Large Animal Clinic.

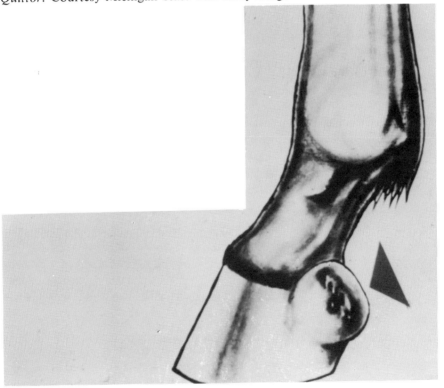

THRUSH

This is a disease affecting the cleft of the frog, generally caused by decomposition of stable manure and other filth that is allowed to collect between the frog and the bars. Severe cases of thrush occasionally produce lameness, but most cases respond well to cleanliness and proper treatment. (See Chapter 9).

STIFLED

The stifle joint is the largest and most complicated joint in the horse's body and is subject to various problems. However, a horse is said to be stifled when the patella of the stifle joint is displaced. If the displacement is toward the outside of the leg, the condition is serious and usually incurable. If the displacement is upward, the patella may be forced back into position.

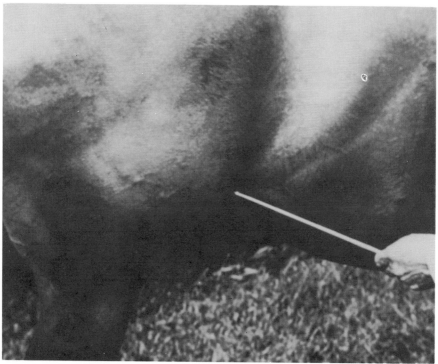

Stifled. Courtesy Michigan State University Large Animal Clinic.

THOROUGHPIN

Thoroughpin is a soft, puffy swelling which appears at the back of the hind leg just above the point of the hock. When pressed with the finger at one side of the limb, it will bulge out on the opposite side. Lameness does not usually occur and most thoroughpins are incurable.

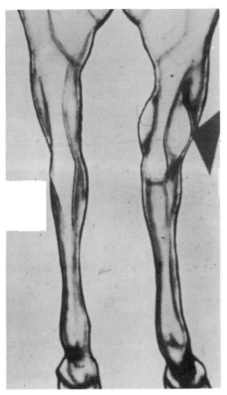

Thoroughpin. Courtesy Michigan State University Large Animal Clinic.

STRINGHALT

Stringhalt has been classified as a nervous disease, but the cause is unknown. It is characterized by a sudden, involuntary flexion of one or both hocks in which the foot is jerked up much higher than normal. The symptoms can be intermittent or so mild that jerking is noticed only occasionally. It can also be so severe that the leg is jerked upward at each step. Some cases can be cured surgically.

BONE OR JACK SPAVIN

Bone spavin is a hard bony growth that may appear on any of the bones which form the hock. However, it is usually found on the inside and lower portions. The cause is not definitely known but is believed to be an hereditary disease. Affected animals should not be used for breeding purposes. Bone spavin is one of the most serious unsoundnesses of the horse.

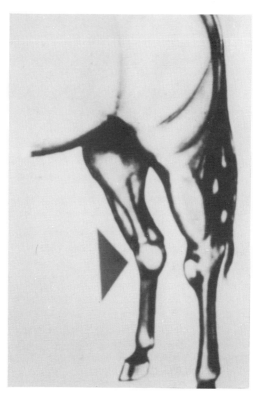

Bog Spavin. Courtesy Michigan State University Large Animal Clinic.

Bone Spavin. Courtesy Michigan State University Large Animal Clinic.

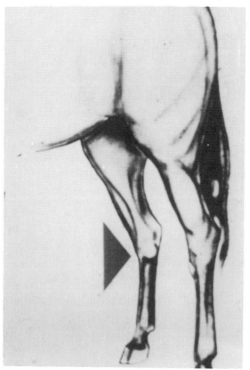

BOG SPAVIN

The bog spavin is fairly common in highly fitted horses. It is a large, soft swelling that usually occurs on the front and inside of the hock. As a rule lameness does not occur unless the distension is so great that it interferes mechanically with the action of the joint.

BLOOD SPAVIN

The blood spavin is caused by the dilation of the large vein that crosses over the front and inside of the hock. It is smaller than the bog spavin, and lameness never occurs.

CAPPED HOCK

Since lameness rarely occurs with the capped hock, the condition is not considered serious. It is a firm swelling that appears on the point of the hock. It may be as large as a tennis ball or so small that it is hardly noticeable. The condition usually results from a constant irritation such as rubbing or kicking the walls of the stall. Thus it may be an indicator of the horse's disposition.

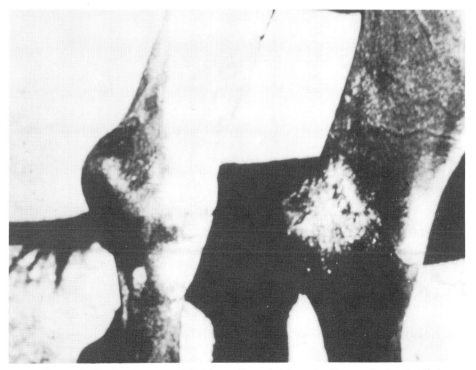

Capped Hock. Courtesy Michigan State University Large Animal Clinic.

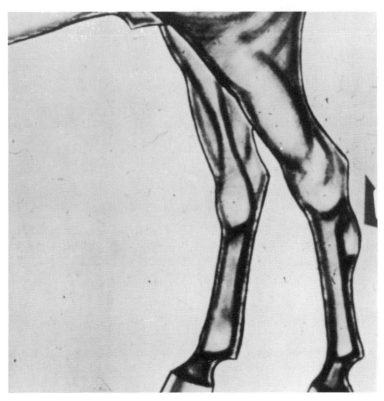

Curb. Courtesy Michigan State University Large Animal Clinic.

CURB

A curb is a hard swelling on the back of the rear cannon bone, about 4 inches below the point of the hock. A large curb is easily seen when looking at the hock and cannon directly from the side. A curb usually follows overexertion or strain, but it may also result from a kick or blow. Crooked hocks are most subject to this unsoundness since the faulty conformation throws a greater strain on the hock. Lameness may disappear after the initial formation of the curb, but the condition must be considered an unsoundness because the affected hock is less likely to endure hard work and severe strain.

THICK WIND

This is a term applied to difficult breathing due to an obstruction of the respiratory tract. The "thick" breathing sound is usually made both on inhaling and exhaling. This condition may be cured if it is possible to remove the obstruction that is blocking the respiratory tract.

ROARING

Roaring is caused by a paralysis of the nerve that passes into the muscles of the larynx. The result is that the muscles atrophy and allow the vocal cords to relax and vibrate as air is inhaled. thus causing the whistling sound that is typical of the "roarer." Some roarers can be cured or improved surgically.

HEAVES, ASTHMA, BROKEN WIND

These conditions of the lungs are incurable, although a veterinarian may prescribe treatment that will restore the usefulness of the horse for a time. Dusty or moldy hay will greatly aggravate these conditions and should be avoided in all horse rations. Heaves is characterized by difficult expiration and a cough and is most often seen in horses more than seven years of age.

14

Care of the Pregnant Mare and the Newborn Foal

Making the decision to breed your mare is not a move you should arrive at without careful consideration. Good breeding is not done simply to propagate the species: the purpose is to improve it. Nature has its own way—survival of the fittest.

Humans have taken horses out of their natural environment and away from nature's carefully planned way, so an intelligent breeding program instituted by humans should be nature's substitute. Therefore breeding with the stallion down the road simply because he is handy and you have decided that your mare ought to have a foal is not good-sense breeding.

Consider two questions before you decide to breed:

1. Do you have adequate facilities for raising a foal? A box stall or dirt feeding lot is not a good place to raise a foal. A foal needs plenty of fresh air and exercise. A good pasture with room to run and develop his muscles will have to be considered a necessity.

2. Is your mare of suitable breeding stock? Be objectively critical in analyzing the qualities of your mare. If she doesn't have many good qualities to pass along to her offspring, reconsider the idea of breeding her. Knowledgeable

breeders attribute only 40 percent of the foal's quality to the stallion; the other 60 percent is the mare's doing.

The purpose of selective breeding is to improve the quality of the horse. That is equally true if your mare is purebred or a grade (mixed-breed) animal.

If your mare is purebred, make it your business to thoroughly investigate her blood lines and breeding. Study your mare's background as well as that of any stallion that you are considering breeding her to. Know any conformation faults your mare may have, and breed away from them.

Do the same thing with the stallion. To breed a low-backed mare to a low-backed stallion would undoubtedly produce a low-backed foal. The same is true with cow hocks or any other conformation fault. It will be time well spent to have a look at other offspring produced by the stallion to see what kind of colts he is parenting.

If your mare is of unknown or mixed breed (grade), look for a purebred stallion to breed her to that is as close to her type as possible. Find a stallion that will add refinement to the foal. If the mare is coarse, you should look for a finer boned stud. If she is too whispy and fine, you should look for a stud with more substance. By no means breed a grade mare to a grade stallion.

The natural breeding season for the mare is in the spring of the year. The usual signs of a mare in season are

1. more frequent urination
2. relaxation of the external genitals
3. the apparent desire for company
4. teasing of other mares
5. mucous discharge from the vagina

Mares generally start coming into season, or "heat," somewhere from twelve to fifteen months of age. However, only exceptionally well-developed fillies should be bred as late two-year-olds, and then they must be fed well in order to provide adequate nutrition for their own immature bodies as well as for the developing fetus. However, it is normally best not to breed the filly until she is at least three years old so that she will foal when she is four. To breed earlier than this takes too much out of the filly.

If brood mares are properly cared for and fed, it is not uncommon for them to produce regularly up to seventeen years of age. In some exceptional cases they may produce foals up to twenty-five years. Proper conditioning of the mare prior to breeding is important. This conditioning consists of adequate and proper feed as well as sufficient exercise.

For the highest rate of conception, mares should be neither too thin nor too fat. The happy medium seems to provide the best results.

Heat periods vary with the individual mare. However, they recur at approximately twenty-one day intervals. The duration of the heat period also varies and may last as long as a month but it is usually somewhere from four to six days. The average gestation period is 336 days, or a little over 11 months. This also varies with individual mares and may be as much as thirty days over or under this period.

Probably the best place to put a pregnant mare is to turn her out to pasture. The pregnant mare is usually sedate. Therefore it is best if she is not pastured with barren or maiden mares who are more apt to run, tease, and kick. Provide adequate shelter to get her out of the severe weather and winter storms. Provide pasture in which shade, fresh water, and a free-choice mineral block are available. Otherwise mares of the light horse breeds should be exercised for an hour each day, up to within a day or two of foaling. Most particularly, do not confine her to a stall or a small dry lot.

The sign indicating the approach of parturition is a distended udder. This will be observed two to six weeks before foaling time. Perhaps seven to ten days before the arrival there will be a marked shrinking or falling away of the muscular parts at the top of the buttocks. Although the udder may have filled out previously, the teats seldom fill out to the ends more than four or five days before foaling, and a waxy substance may form on them.

A week or so before the estimated foaling date it is a good idea to check with your veterinarian and make sure he is going to be available in the event you have need of him. If he is not, get the telephone number of another veterinarian you may call.

As foaling time draws near, milk may drip from the teats and the mare will show restlessness. She will more than likely break into a sweat, lie down, and get up repeatedly.

Mares are very individual when it comes to the birthing process. They insist upon doing it their way. Some mares will follow the prescribed ritual; others may simply produce their foal when least expected. Therefore it is well to be prepared as much as thirty days in advance of the expected foaling date.

WHAT TO DO AT FOALING TIME

An attendant should be on hand for a mare delivering a foal for the first time, for an old mare or for a mare in poor condition. A good rule

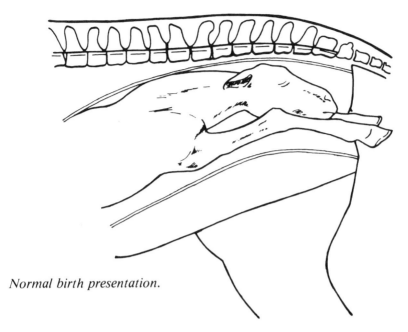

Normal birth presentation.

is to be near, but not in sight. Some mares resent an intrusion on their privacy at this time and will actually delay foaling as long as possible when being watched. It is not uncommon for a mare to wait for the attendant to go up to the house for a hot cup of coffee before concluding the business of foaling.

The purpose of the attendant at foaling time is to prevent possible injury to the mare and foal and to call a competent veterinarian if necessary. Only a very experienced attendant should attempt to help the mare if she is having difficulty in delivering. A well meaning but foolish amateur can cause irreparable damage.

The first indication that the mare is actually foaling is the rupture of the outer fetal membrane, followed by the expulsion of a large amount of fluid. This is often referred to as the bursting of the water bag. Next the inner membrane surrounding the foal appears, and labor becomes more marked.

In normal delivery the mare foals rapidly, usually within five to thirty minutes. When the labor contractions are at their height, the mare will lie down. At the time the foal is born, the mare will be lying on her side.

In the normal birth presentation, the front feet with heels down come first followed by the nose, which is positioned on top of them. Then come the shoulders, the middle, the hips, the hind legs, and the feet. Feet presented with the bottoms up indicate they are the hind ones, and there is likely to be difficulty. If the presentation is other than normal, a veterinarian should be called at once, because there is greater danger that the foal will smother if birth is delayed.

After foaling, make certain that the foal is breathing and that the membrane has been removed from his mouth and nostrils. Then let the mare and foal rest quietly as long as possible to gain strength.

At this time the mare will be touching the foal with her nose and licking him with her tongue. Don't interfere with this moment, particularly with the first time mother. She is picking up her own scent on the foal and trying to figure out what it is.

Shortly after the foal has arrived it should be thoroughly rubbed and dried with warm towels and moved to a corner of the stall on clean, fresh straw. The mare will be less restless if the foal is in her line of vision.

During the birth process or shortly thereafter, the umbilical cord will usually break of its own accord. To reduce the danger of navel infection (navel ill or joint ill) the navel cord of the foal should be treated at once with iodine. Many horsepeople prefer to use an organic or "tamed" iodine such as povidone. It has all the chemical properties of tincture of iodine but does not burn or irritate the foal's sensitive skin.

Treating the navel is best done while the foal is still lying down. Place the end of the cord to a wide-mouthed bottle nearly full of iodine, and press the bottle firmly against the foal's abdomen. Dust the cord with antiseptic powder, and repeat this process daily until the stump dries up and falls off (usually three or four days). As an added precautionary measure, also treat the bottom of the foal's feet with iodine.

Protect the eyes of the newborn foal from bright light. As soon as the mare and foal are up, clean the stall. Wet, stained, or soiled bedding should be removed. Sprinkle the floor lightly with lime, and provide clean, fresh bedding.

After foaling the mare is frequently somewhat hot and feverish. Offer her small quantities of lukewarm water at intervals, but do not allow her to gorge.

If the weather is extremely cold and the mare is hot and sweaty, she should be well rubbed down, dried and blanketed soon after getting on her feet. In cold weather a heat lamp is a valuable aid in keeping the mare and foal comfortable.

If the placenta (afterbirth) is not expelled by the time the mare gets up, it should either be tied up in a knot or tied to her tail. This eliminates the possibility of either the mare or foal stepping on it and increasing the danger of inflammation of the uterus and foal founder in the mare. Usually the placenta will be expelled soon after foaling. If it is retained for more than two hours, call the veterinarian. Be alert for any difficulties that may develop. The mare's normal temperature is about 100 degrees. If it is much above that, something is wrong.

The strong, healthy foal should be up on his feet and ready to nurse within two hours. Sometimes, however, the big awkward foal will need a little help and guidance during his first attempts at nursing. He knows what he's supposed to be doing, he just doesn't always know how to get the job done. Before the foal nurses for the first time, wash the mare's udder with a mild disinfectant and rinse it with clean, warm water.

COLOSTRUM

Make very certain that the newborn foal secures the first milk, which contains colostrum. Because of the importance of colostrum, mares should never be milked out prior to foaling. If the foal is very weak, he may nurse the mare if he is steadied by an attendant. The milk also can be drawn from the mare and fed to the foal by nursing bottle for a few times.

Colostrum is important because it has the following functions:

1. It contains antibodies that temporarily protect the foal against certain infection, especially of the digestive tract.
2. It serves as a natural purgative, removing fecal matter that has become accumulated in the digestive tract during gestation.

Regulating the foal's bowel movement is very important. Constipation and scours (diarrhea) are common ailments.

Material called meconium, which is impacted in the bowels during fetal development, may kill the foal if it is not eliminated properly. Usually a good feed of colostrum will cause natural elimination. However, this is not always the case.

Observe the foal's bowel movement from four to six hours after birth. If there has been no fecal discharge by this time, an enema may be in order. A fleet enema purchased from your drugstore is very suitable, or use one to two quarts of warm soapy water (101 degrees) or one to two quarts of warm water mixed with a little glycerin. Inject the solution into the foal's rectum with a baby syringe that has about a 3-inch nipple. Repeat the treatment until normal yellow feces appear.

If the foal is scouring (diarrhea), reduce the mare's grain ration and take away part of her milk by milking her out at intervals.

Scours also may result from infectious disease or dirty surroundings, contaminated udder or teats, nonremoval of fecal matter from the digestive tract, fretfulness or elevated temperature in the mare, too much feed affecting the quality of the mare's milk, a cold damp bed, or continued exposure to cold rains or weather. Consult your veterinarian for treatment.

PREVENTATIVE SHOTS FOR MARE AND FOAL

Ideally your mare should have a tetanus toxoid booster about two months before foaling. This will create a high level of active immunity in her body which she will pass to the foal through the colostrum. At the time of birth, the foal should immediately have an antitoxin shot. At three months of age the foal should receive his first tetanus toxoid shot, followed by a second tetanus toxoid shot in four to six weeks. After that he can go on a once-a-year tetanus toxoid booster.

If the tetanus status of the mare is unknown, she should receive a tetanus toxoid shot at the time of the delivery, and the foal should receive an antitoxin shot.

Many veterinarians routinely give the mare an antibiotic shot following the delivery. This is a precautionary measure against infection caused by any retained placental material.

It is wise to consult your veterinarian about viral abortion shots prior to breeding your mare. Follow his or her recommendation.

MASTITIS

To prevent mastitis in the mare and diarrhea in the foal keep the mare off grain for a week before and after foaling. If your mare is a big grain eater, give her only a handful of oats and bran to keep her happy. Ease her gradually back onto grain about a week after foaling.

CARE OF THE SUCKLING FOAL

There is no better place for a mare and foal than in a pasture, weather conditions permitting. When the foal is only a few days old he will begin to nibble on a little grass, hay, or grain. To promote development and avoid any setback at weaning time, the foal should be encouraged to eat supplementary feed as early as possible. In most mares the production of milk drops off drastically when the foal is six to eight weeks old, so it is well to have the foal established on solid food prior to that time. The average weaning age is four months.

Provide a low-built grain box or "creep" especially for the foal. It is necessary to make this provision or the mare will eat her ration and the foal's too. There are many good commercial feeds formulated especially for the foal's needs. Rolled oats and wheat bran with a little brown sugar added is especially palatable as a starting ration. Cracked corn with a little linseed oil or soybean oil meal may be provided later with good results.

Provide the foal with good hay or pasture in addition to its grain rations. A healthy foal should be eating a half-pound of grain daily per 100 pounds of body weight at four to five weeks of age. This amount should be increased by weaning time to about three-fourths of a pound or more per 100 pounds of body weight. The exact amount varies with the individual foal, the type of feed, and the development desired.

Under such a system, by the time the foal reaches his first year he should have attained one-half of his mature weight. By the time he reaches his second year he should be at or near his full height. Such results require liberal feeding from the start. A foal stunted in his first year by insufficient feeding cannot be developed properly later in life.

BREEDING THE MARE "BACK" AFTER FOALING

After foaling, the mare comes into "foal heat" at about nine days. An increasing number of good horsepeople do not attempt to rebreed the mare on this heat, but wait for the heat period following the foal heat, between the twenty-fifth and thirtieth day from foaling.

Often the foal shows signs of foal-heat scours (diarrhea) when it is seven to ten days old. This is common and usually clears up on its own within several days.

15
Personal Safety around the Horse

Few animals can match the horse in size and strength. However, humans have the advantage of being able to think and act readily. Therefore, it behooves the wise horse person to think when he or she is working with or is around the horse. It does little good to voice the words "I didn't think" after an unfortunate incident has happened. The time to think is before.

The following remarks vary in content, but they have at least one thing in common: they concern incidents to which the "I didn't think" response is frequently voiced by the novice horse person.

1. Steady a frightened horse. Don't punish him. If he is already upset, punishment will only make the situation worse.

2. Improperly used pesticides can be injurious to humans, animals, and plants. Follow the directions on the label, and heed all precautions as stated.

3. Store pesticides, repellents, and rodent bait out of the reach of children and animals, preferably under lock and key.

4. Be sure your riding equipment is in good condition and repair. A girth or stirrup leather that breaks while you are riding can be more than an inconvenience. It can be the source of a bad accident.

5. Always recheck your girth before mounting. You don't want it so tight that the horse is uncomfortable, but neither do you want it slipping.

6. Be sure your bridle is properly adjusted and fitted to the horse. You'd be surprised how many neophyte horsepeople manage to get them on backwards.

7. When saddling the horse, you should make sure the hair under the saddle pad is smooth and that no hair is caught in the cinch or girth. The pad is supposed to offer protection, not be a source of irritation. A hurting horse can be a fractious one.

8. Wear boots for riding. They afford good support for the feet and ankles. Tennis shoes are great for athletics, but in the stirrups it's too easy for the feet to slide through and get caught.

9. Wear sturdy shoes or boots when working around the horse. You have invited trouble if your horse steps on your big toe while you are wearing a pair of sandals.

10. Do not smoke in the stable or near stored grain, hay, or straw. All of these materials are very dry and may ignite easily.

11. Always carry a crop or stick when walking through a pasture with horses in it. Horses are curious and playful, and they play horse fashion, not people fashion. When engaged in play it is natural for a horse to rear, nip, strike, and kick. If by chance the horses are closely attuned to you, it is more than likely that they will also be jealous if you should stop and pet another horse, and they will react accordingly.

12. Do not pet the horse on the nose. This will encourage nipping. Pet him on the neck or shoulder.

13. Avoid making sudden loud noises around the horse. He is easily startled.

14. Approach a strange horse with caution. You don't know his habits, and he may have some bad ones.

15. When riding in the company of other horses, allow sufficient distance between the animals to avoid kicking.

16. In riding uphill or down, allow the horse his head for balance.

17. Do not wear clothing that flaps around the horse. A long flowing scarf may be attractive, but it can spook a horse.

18. Watch out for small children and pets around horses. Near the horses feet is not a safe place to play.

19. Always walk your horse on concrete or hard-surfaced roads.

20. You are liable for any damage caused by your horse. This includes bodily harm, automobile accidents, or property damage done by an escaped horse.

21. The position of the horse's ears is an excellent barometer as to how he feels and what he is thinking. If they are plastered back, and flat against his head, he is angry at something. Do not get between the horse and the source of his anger.

22. If you do not know how to properly ride a horse, take lessons from a competent teacher. If you do not know how to tell the horse what to do, there is no way he can guess it.

23. Spurs can be a useful aid to someone who knows how to use them. However, the indiscriminate use of spurs can quickly turn a rider into a pedestrian.

24. Do not pester your horse when he is eating. To the horse, food time is his favorite period. Although many horses do not appear to be disturbed by interference, some individuals may bite.

25. When they are not in use, always put away tools such as pitchforks and rakes. If they are left carelessly in the aisle, they can be dangerous instruments to people and to horses.

26. When riding or handling a horse, especially in strange surroundings, stay alert to things that may frighten him. Having the novice horse person and the horse both startled at the same time could cause a rough moment.

27. Displays of anger or emotional outbursts have no place in handling or training the horse

28. The wise horseperson will keep his mind awake and his body in a well-balanced position when handling and working around the horse. Should something unexpected happen, he will be able to move quickly.

29. Never rush into a stall, touch the horse, or stand behind him without first speaking or letting him know of your presence. To do so might startle him and could result in a kick for the thoughtless person.

30. When riding through the fields or woods during hunting season, make sure you are highly visible and audible. Wear bright-colored clothing and even go so far as to attach a bell to your saddle. More than one horse has been mistaken for a pheasant.

31. Watch freshly cured hay carefully for heat. There is always the possibility of spontaneous combustion.

32. Always walk your horse back to the barn from a ride. It will help cool him out, and prevent you from becoming a "headless horseman" when he bolts in the barn door.

33. Avoid trouble. It is infinitely easier and safer than trying to get out of it.

34. If you are having problems riding or handling your horse, you need help from a competent horseperson. Don't be shy in seeking help. Ask your veterinarian or farrier or a respected horseperson of your acquaintance. Chances are he or she will be able to refer you to someone who can be of assistance.

35. Pick the right spot for mounting your horse. Never mount in a small barn or near fences, trees, or overhanging projections.

36. If your horse is frightened by an object, dismount and lead him past it.

37. Horses are easily frightened by unusual objects and noises. Anticipate these, and steady your horse.

38. Maintain a secure seat when riding, and keep your horse under control at all times.

39. If your horse becomes frightened and attempts to run, turn him in a circle and tighten it until he stops.

16
History and Breeds

The origin and prehistory of the horse is open to some speculation and controversy by the experts. Some trace equine ancestry to the Great Plains region of North America. Others contend it was Central Asia. However, they do agree that he evolved in three stages to his present form.

The original eohippus, dating back some 58 million years, was only about 12 inches high. He had four toes on each front foot, three toes on each hind foot, a short neck, and even teeth and was adapted to living in a forested and swampy environment.

As the earth underwent geologic changes, so did the horse. He evolved into his second stage, mesohippus. He became larger, about 24 inches high, and developed teeth suitable for grazing. His longer legs, with only three toes on each foot, afforded him greater speed and endurance for protection and survival and for finding forage and water.

The third and final stage in the evolution of the horse is his present form, equus. For reasons yet unknown, this species completely died out in North America. Therefore, it was in Asia and Europe that the horse completed his development. The horse did not return to North America until the sixteenth century, when he was brought here by the Spaniards.

The horse thrived in the new land, and the people who lived here bred and developed horses to meet their own particular needs. New breeds, such as the American Saddle Horse, the Morgan, the Tennessee Walking Horse, the Quarter Horse, the Appaloosa, and the Standardbred, came into being.

During the industrial and mechanical revolution in the United States the horse, no longer a necessity as a beast of burden, became obsolete. The tractor replaced the draft horse, the automobile replaced the light breeds, and the number of horses was drastically reduced.

However, according to a recent survey the number of horses in the United States today is well over 6 million. This is more than double the number recorded in 1960. In fact these figures indicate that the light horses are the fastest growing segment of the livestock industry in the country. Horse shows are increasing in size and number, and saddle clubs are growing in membership. Projects in the 4-H Horse Clubs outnumber projects in 4-H Beef Clubs. More people are riding horses for pleasure than ever before.

CLASSIFICATION OF HORSES

Horses may be classified as ponies, light horses, or draft horses. They are designated and classified according to size, build, and use.

A hand is the standard measure of height for horses. The term is a hold-over from the days when it was not practical to carry around a stick to measure horses. The average width of a man's hand was four inches so this was established as a ruler. The horse is measured in a straight line from the point of the withers to the ground. Thus an animal that measures sixty inches from withers to ground would be a 15 hand horse. An animal measuring sixty-two inches would be 15.2 hands.

Light horses stand 14.2 to 17 hands and weight 900 to 1,400 pounds. Their primary use is for riding, driving, showing, racing, or for utility purposes on the farm. Light horses are more rangy and capable of more action and speed than draft horses.

Draft horses stand 14.2 to 17.2 hands and weight 1,400 pounds or more. They are primarily used for drawing loads and other heavy work. However, they are rapidly becoming popular attractions in the show ring.

BREEDS OF HORSES

A breed can be defined as a group of horses possessing certain well-defined, distinctive, uniformly transmitted characteristics not common to other horses and having a common origin.

Some of the popular breeds of light horses are discussed below.

American Saddle Horse

The American Saddle Horse was developed by the pioneers of Kentucky who desired a utility horse of beauty, easy gaits, gentle even temperament, substance, quality, and stamina. Such a horse was first known as a Kentucky Saddler.

The coloring may be bay, chestnut, black, or gray with an occasional roan. The average height is 15 to 16 hands, and weight is from 1,000 to 1,200 pounds. White markings on the head and legs are common. However, gaudy white markings are undesirable. The animal has a long graceful neck and proud bearing with long sloping pasterns which provide the springiness so necessary for a smooth, comfortable ride. The American Saddle Horse is used as a three-and five-gaited show horse, harness, pleasure, stock, and trail horse.

American Saddle Horse. Photo of Prim Style. Courtesy of Mr. and Mrs. William G. Blacklaw.

Appaloosa

Appaloosa horses originated in the northwestern United States. They have variable coat coloring, usually with white over the loin and hips and round or egg-shaped dark spots on the white area. The "leopard" Appaloosa coloring has small spots over the entire body. The skin is mottled, the hoofs are striped vertically black and white, and the eyes show more white than most breeds. Appaloosas are used as pleasure, stock, parade, and race horses.

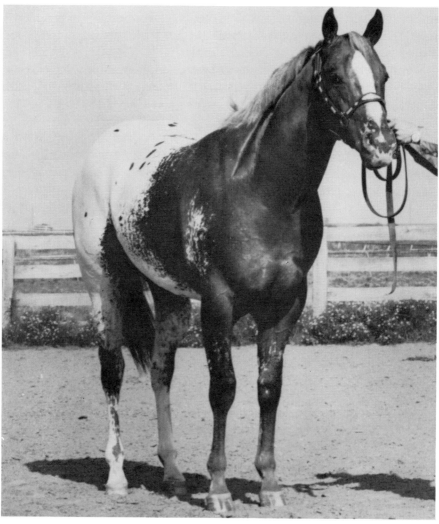

Appaloosa. Photo of Bar Plaudit. Courtesy of Mr. and Mrs. Billy Williams and Appaloosa Horse Club, Inc.

Arabian. Courtesy of Dr. and Mrs. James Rooker.

Arabian

Arabian horses originated in the desert of Arabia where climactic conditions alone would tend to develop a hardy, enduring breed. The coat colors are bay, gray, chestnut and occasionally white or black. The profile of the head is straight, or preferably slightly concave below the eyes, with a small muzzle, large nostrils, and large, round, dark eyes. White markings on the head and legs are common, the skin is always dark. Height is from 14.1 to 15.1 hands, with an occasional individual over or under. They are used as stock, show, race, parade, and pleasure horses.

Morgan

The Morgan horses originated in the northeastern United States. Their height is 14.2 to 15.2 hands with some individuals over or under. Their weight is from 900 to 1,100 pounds. The coat colors are bay, chestnut, brown, or black, and extensive white markings are uncom-

Morgan. Photo of Shaker's Gazon. Courtesy of Mr. and Mrs. James Darling.

mon. In general the Morgan is compact, of medium length, well-muscled, smooth, and stylish in appearance.

Animals are disqualified for registration if they have wall-eyes or have white leg markings above the knee or hock. They are used as show, pleasure, stock horses and are also shown under harness.

Palomino

Palomino is a word designating color rather than a specific breed. Therefore a Palomino horse may be any breed or combination of breeds. They are the "golden" horses. They have light-colored manes and tails of white, silver, or ivory. The mane and tail may not have more than 15 percent dark or chestnut hair. White markings on the legs and face are common. Palomino horses originated in the United States from animals of Spanish extraction. The ideal coat of the Palomino is described as "the color of a newly minted copper penny." They are used as stock, show, parade, and pleasure horses.

Palomino. Photo of McClure's Shady Lady (double registered Palomino-American Saddle Horse). Courtesy Mr. and Mrs. Robert K. McClure.

Pinto

Pinto horses originated in the United States but are descendants of the Spanish horses brought here by the conquistadores. The word "Pinto" designates color markings. Therefore, a Pinto horse may be any breed or combination of breeds as long as the coat coloring meets specific requirements.

To be eligible for registration the minimum height of the mature Pinto is 14.0 hands. The ideal Pinto has a 50-50 color pattern distribution. However, the patterns and markings are extremely varied and found in many colors. The two distinct pattern markings are "overo" and "tobiano." Overo is a colored horse with white areas extending upward from the belly and lower regions, and there may be other white markings. On a tobiano the white areas on the back extend downward and there may be other white markings as well.

"Glass" eyes are acceptable for registry. Pintos are used for show, parade, pleasure, and stock work.

Pinto. Photo of Fisty's Poco Miss. Courtesy of Mrs. Verna L. Milby.

Quarter Horse

As a breed Quarter Horses originated in the United States. These horses are well muscled and powerfully built. They have small alert ears and heavily muscled cheeks and jaws. Their coloring is chestnut, bay, dun, roan, black, palomino, or brown. For registration the animals are disqualified if they have pinto, Appaloosa, or albino coloring or white marking on the underline. They are used as pleasure, show, stock, cutting, and race horses.

Quarter horse. Courtesy American Quarter Horse Association.

Standardbred

Standardbred horses originated in the United States. They are smaller, less leggy, and more rugged than Thoroughbreds. The most common colors are brown, chestnut, black, bay, and occasionally gray, roan, or dun. They are used for harness racing, either trotting or pacing, and in certain harness classes at horse shows.

Tennessee Walking Horse

The Tennessee Walking Horse was developed in the Central Basin of Tennessee. The horse stands 15 to 16 hands high, with an occasional individual over or under, and weighs 1,000 to 1,200 pounds. The most common coat colors are chestnut, black, roan, bay, brown and gray, with an occasional white or palomino. White markings on the face and legs are common.

The Tennessee Walking Horse is characterized by a flat walk and running walk, with a typical "nodding" of the head with each step.

Standardbred. Photo of Adios Cleo. Courtesy Shiawassee Farm, Inc.

Tennessee Walking Horse. Photo of Black Dust M.R. Courtesy Miss Betty Sain and Tennessee Walking Horse Breeders' and Exhibitors Associations.

Thoroughbred

The Thoroughbred originated in England and is noted for fineness of conformation and long, straight, well-muscled legs. Coat colors are bay, brown, chestnut, black, and occasionally roan or gray. White markings on the face and legs are common.

Thoroughbred horses are commonly used as hunters, jumpers, and saddle, stock, polo, or race horses.

Thoroughbred. Photo of Scooter T. Courtesy Ms. Jeane Metsker.

17
Breed Registry Associations

American Albino Association, Inc.—*named changed to:* World Wide Cream and White Registry, Box 79, Crabtree, Oregon, 97335.

American Association of Owners and Breeders of Peruvian Paso Horses, Post Office Box 371, Calabasa, California, 91302.

American Buckskin Registry Association, Post Office Box 1125, Anderson, California, 96007.

American Connermara Pony Society, Route 2, Featherbed Lane, Ballston Spa, New York, 12020.

American Gotland Horse Association, Rural Route No. 2, Elkland, Missouri, 65644.

American Hackney Horse Society, 527 Madison Avenue, Room 725, New York, New York, 10022.

American Morgan Horse Association, Inc., Oneida County Airport Industrial Park, Box 1, Westmoreland, New York, 13490.

American Mustang Association, Inc., 997 South Douglas Street, Calimesa, California, 92320.

American Paint Horse Association, Post Office Box 12487, Fort Worth, Texas, 76116.

American Paso Fino Pleasure Horse Association, Inc., Arrott Building, 401 Wood Street, Pittsburgh, Pennsylvania, 15222.

American Quarter Horse Association, Post Office Box 200, Amarillo, Texas, 79168.

American Remount Association, 20560 Perris Boulevard, Perris, California, 92370 (Half-Thoroughbred Registry).

American Saddle Horse Breeders Association, 929 South Fourth Street, Louisville, Kentucky, 40203.

American Shetland Pony Club, Post Office Box 2339, West Lafayette, Indiana, 47920.

Appaloosa Horse Club, Inc., Box 8403, Moscow, Idaho, 83843.

Arabian Horse Club Registry of America, 3435 S. Yosimite Street, Denver, Colorado, 80110.

Cleveland Bay Society of America, White Post, Virginia, 22663.

Galiceno Horse Breeders Association, Inc., 111 E. Elm Street, Tyler, Texas, 75701.

Half-Saddlebred Registry of America, 660 Poplar Street, Coshocton, Ohio, 43812.

Hungarian Horse Association, Bitterroot Stock Farm, Hamilton, Montana, 59840.

International Arabian Horse Association, 224 East Olive Avenue, Burbank California, 91503.

The Jockey Club, 300 Park Avenue, New York, New York, 10022 (Thoroughbred horses).

Missouri Fox Trotting Horse Breed Association, Inc., Post Office Box 637, Ava, Missouri, 65608.

Morocco Spotted Horse Cooperative Association of America, Route 1, Ridott, Illinois, 61067.

Palomino Horse Association, Box 128, Chatsworth, California, 91311.

Palomino Horse Breeders of America, Post Office Box 249, Mineral Wells, Texas, 76067.

Pinto Horse Association of America, Inc., 7525 Mission Gorge Road, Suite C, San Diego, California, 92120.

Pony of the Americas Club, Inc., Post Office Box 1447, Mason City, Iowa, 50401.

Spanish Mustang Registry, Inc., Cayuse Ranch, Oshoto, Wyoming, 82724.

Tennessee Walking Horse Breeder's Association of America, Post Office Box 286, Lewisburg, Tennessee, 37091.

The United States Trotting Association, 750 Michigan Avenue, Columbus, Ohio, 43215.

Welsh Pony Society of America, Inc., 202 North Chester Street, West Chester, Pennsylvania, 19308.

Indexes

INDEX TO TEXT

132

INDEX TO ILLUSTRATIONS AND TABLES